W9-BDW-674

Them, Us & Me:

How the Old Testament speaks to people today

Randall

May you be blessed
& inspired by this book

Jacqui Young

Them, Us & Me:

How the Old Testament speaks to people today

Jacqueline Grey

APSS Vol. 2

APSS & SCD Press
Sydney, Australia

2007

Author Details

Jacqueline Nancye Grey
1974-

Sydney College of Divinity Press
P.O. Box 1882, Macquarie Centre,
NSW 2113 Australia

Cover design: Stephen Wall, 2008
www.helloyelo.info
Featured artwork on cover: Jane Latella, 2007
Author Photograph: Amber Jones, 2008
Layout: Mark Hutchinson
Maps and Illustrations: Jacqueline Grey

Them, Us & Me: How the Old Testament speaks to people today
Copyright©2008 by Jacqueline Grey

Cataloguing in Publication:
Author: Grey, Jacqueline Nancye, 1974 -
Title: Them, Us & Me: How the Old Testament speaks to people today.
Edition: 1st ed.
Publisher: Macquarie Centre, N.S.W.: Sydney College of Divinity, 2008.
ISBN: 978-1-920770-03-7 (pbk.):
Subjects: Old Testament - Hermeneutics
               Pentecostalism - Thought.
Other Authors: Sydney College of Divinity.
Dewey Number: 230.0711

CONTENTS

FOREWORD

Pentecostal and charismatic communities have long been suspicious of theologians, favouring a spirituality of the heart and not the head. It is not uncommon, even in our more modern churches, to hear criticism of academics from the pulpit, with declarations that scholars deal with little more than incomprehensible abstractions, ignoring the more day to day needs and concerns of the average person in the pew (if such a person actually exits). No doubt, such attitudes do most academics an injustice, yet it is the case that many of the books written by scholars are directed at their colleagues, and while not antithetical to faith, these texts are certainly difficult to understand. *Them, Us & Me* is one of the exceptions to this tendency.

Informed by Jacqui's doctoral studies, which addressed the topic of Pentecostal hermeneutics of the Old Testament, this book is grounded in thorough research and intelligent analysis. Yet those who pick up this book are hardly likely to be aware of this background, because the text itself is eminently readable, easy to understand, and directed, not to the academy, but to the person in the pew. Anyone who desires to understand the ancient and seemingly difficult Old Testament text will be delighted with this book. Jacqui does not patronise her audience, presuming that they are shallow and illiterate, but neither does she confuse and confound them with difficult language and profoundly incomprehensible concepts. Rather, she provides them with the requisite tools to understand and read the Scriptures for themselves. In so doing, *Them, Us & Me* becomes a book that combines theory and practical spirituality.

This book is the second of the *Australasian Pentecostals Studies* (APS) supplementary series. Under the sponsorship of Southern Cross College, the underlying purpose of APS is to encourage and facilitate Pentecostal thinking and scholarship in the Australasian region. With the inaugural issue being published in March 1998, the APS journal has more than contributed to this goal, publishing noteworthy articles from local scholars as well as contributions from internationally recognized academics. In 1999 the first book in the supplementary series was released – *Pelegrini: An Italian Protestant Community in Sydney (1958-1998)*, written by Mark Hutchinson. This second book is intended to be the first of many more, as APS ramps up its book publishing, and provides a vehicle for Pentecostal scholars to contribute their particular gifts to the church.

SHANE CLIFTON, PhD

Editor: *Australasian Pentecostal Studies journal*

Academic Dean, Southern Cross College

PREFACE

Growing up in a Christian family in greater Sydney I came to love the stories of the Old Testament. This love has never dulled. It led me to theological college to pursue this interest. That same passion for studying the bible then led me into teaching and research. It is a joy and privilege to see students understand and treasure the Old Testament. That same passion has led me to write this book. In this love of the bible, I hope (like Peter Pan) to never grow up!

In the preparation to publish this book, numerous people have asked how long it took to write. It is a difficult question to answer. To say that it has taken "all my life" seems clichéd, but there is an element of truth in that comment. The life-long reading and love of the bible, the years of academic training and study, as well as dedicated time to actually write it have all contributed to the following pages. A lot of the ideas have come out of the research of my doctoral thesis as well as classroom teaching. However probably the most motivating factor was the deep desire to help readers of the Old Testament to not just love it, but understand it. I hope I have achieved that purpose.

Yet while my name appears on the front cover, there are lots of people who have contributed directly and indirectly to this book. I would like to take this opportunity to thank them. There are those who have contributed to the actual production of the book, most of whom are colleagues at Southern Cross College. Mark Hutchinson, who encouraged, formatted and edited it. Narelle Melton who assisted in editing and Stephen Wall who provided the cover design. The cover design is intended to reflect the content of the book and idea of *them, us & me*. The ancient text (represented by the artwork) is being considered by both the Christian community (group of friends standing) and the individual reader (man thinking).

The opportunity to produce the manuscript was only made possible through the provision of a sabbatical from Southern Cross College, of which I am extremely grateful. Throughout this process I have also been encouraged by my colleagues and friends: Dr Shane Clifton, Ps Stephen Fogarty, Dr David Parker, Dr Chris Simon and other staff of the College.

While this book is not a direct result of my doctoral studies, a lot of the ideas have flowed out of that work. Those studies were made possible due to the support of the staff and programs of Charles Sturt University. In the course of that study, I benefited from the financial sponsorship of the Charles Sturt University post-graduate program, for which I am also grateful.

Finally, I would like to acknowledge and thank my close friends, house-mates and family for their grace and patience to me throughout this process. Their continual encouragement and inspiration has been a beacon of hope. In particular, I'd like to thank my parents, John and Nancye Grey – my biggest supporters and promoters of this book!

Please drink of this book... and enjoy responsibly!

JACQUI GREY, PhD
Sydney 2008

Chapter 1

BEGINNING TO READ THE OLD TESTAMENT

When most people pick up their bible and sit down to read it, they want to understand what the book is saying. I think one of the most dissatisfying experiences of reading the Old Testament is knowing that I have just read something profound and insightful, but I just don't know what it was! I've read it, and I know that there's more, but I just don't know how to get it. It's like staring at a famous painting such as the Mona Lisa, knowing that you should be impressed, but not sure exactly why.

The Old Testament makes up over three-quarters of the bible, yet if we're honest with ourselves, we don't always read all of it. Yes, this is time for true confessions. When I was recently reading the 'Bible in a Year', I skipped all the lists of family heritage (genealogies) in Chronicles. We may read the easy parts and sections we feel comfortable with - like the faith-building stories, worshipful Psalms and practical Proverbs - but we don't pay more than a fleeting visit to bits like Leviticus! But why is that? Why don't we read all of it? Why do we avoid sections like the civil law policies on what to do if your house has mould? Sometimes we avoid them because they're boring(!) or seem irrelevant. Sometimes we avoid them because we don't understand them. I hope that through reading this book, you will not only be surprised at the radical importance of the Old Testament for all people, but this will help you discover *how* to read it – even the challenging parts!

This book is about how to effectively read the Old Testament. It will give you some simple keys to understand the bible and apply it to your daily life. It will inspire you to love and value the Old Testament. While it draws on all the experience and knowledge that I have gathered as a teacher and lover of the bible, it is not meant to be *just* an academic textbook. Rather, it is a practical book that is designed to help you to become a confident reader of the Old Testament. By utilising the principles in this book, it will provide you with a practical, commonsense guide on how to *really* understand the bible. It's not difficult, but it does require you to action it. It will also give you a 'big picture' account of the major events and history of the Old Testament to help see where the smaller sections fit into the overall picture. So whether you are a newcomer to the bible or are a seasoned veteran, you will be equipped to read and appreciate the Old Testament for your own devotions and spiritual life as well as your ministry in helping others.

WHY DO WE READ THE OLD TESTAMENT?

When most people pick up their Old Testament and sit down to read it, they do so for a purpose. That purpose may be different for each one of us. Some people just want to comprehend the culture and history of the passage. Other people want to receive guidance and practical insight for their own life. Maybe you read it because you want to know fully who God is and how God acts in the world. Or maybe you read it because you want to meet with that God and be transformed. If you are like me, then you read it for all of the above reasons!

Whatever motivation you have, you are sharing in a noble and historic task. All through the ages, people just like you and me have wept, laughed and wrestled with the same stories and poems found in our Old Testament. Throughout history, the bible has been explored and mined for treasures by scholars and lay readers alike. According to the Reformers (think Martin Luther onwards), there is a "perspicuity" of Scripture. That is, the bible can be read and understood by all people without the requirement of a priest, pope or professor to interpret it for us. This does not mean that we can't learn tools of study to help us read it better or appreciate the interpretations of others around us. Just because something is simple does not mean it is simplistic. What it does mean is that the bible is not the exclusive domain of scholars, but is for everyone. Therefore everyone can and should read it for their personal enrichment and that of their community. While we will discuss exactly what the 'Old Testament' is in the next chapter, the question here is: *how* do we read it? That is the purpose of this book – to empower you to read the Old Testament for yourself.

How THIS BOOK WILL HELP YOU....

This book will help you to be a better reader of the Old Testament by giving you tools to uncover the wealth and treasure that is found in its pages. And like digging for gold, it sometimes requires hard work and thoughtfulness. In Part I, these tools of the trade are outlined and explained. In Part II, we will journey through the basic content of the Old Testament. This will give the 'big picture' of the major events and ideas. As we journey through this basic content we will begin to apply these tools (from Part I) and uncover the wealth of the bible together.

These tools of the trade can be summarised in three strategic questions that you can ask of each passage whenever you want to dig for its gold. And depending on your background knowledge of the bible and commitment to investigation, you can explore these questions according to whatever level of detail you desire. This means that when you sit down to read a passage or consider a concept from the Old Testament, you need to ask three vital questions:

1.   What is the significance of this for *them*?
2.   What is the significance of this for *us*?
3.   What is the significance of this for *me*?

Who is *them*? They are the original hearers of the Old Testament. In other words, *them* is the ancient Israelite community before the coming of Jesus Christ. This is important because it reminds us that the bible is not merely a textbook of human history, but the testimony of God's relationship with humanity that began at creation. In the development of salvation which climaxed at the cross, ancient Israel has played a central role. Jesus was part of a family and a nation that had a long history of relationship with God. So the Old Testament presents the testimony of Israel and their interaction with God. We need to hear this testimony in its own right and appreciate what this ancient witness tells us in their own words. It is this overall testimony of ancient Israel that provides us with the 'big picture' of what the Old Testament is all about in Part II.

Through this testimony of ancient Israel, we observe God's workings. We know and understand the character of God through the record of this testimony of ancient Israel. For example, in Genesis 12:2-3 God gives a promise to Abraham (his name at this point is actually Abram, but to save confusion we will just call him Abraham). God promises to bless him, multiply him and through his seed all the nations of the earth will be blessed. This promise to Abraham is significant to *them* (the Old Testament community) because it became the foundation of their identity as a nation. It also emphasised that ancient Israel was chosen, or elected, to be set apart from the other nations as the vehicle of God's revelation and grace (this is discussed further in chapter 3). But we also understand the Old Testament as being significant to *them* as it was a product of its time - it is a testimony that was written in a particular time and place (this will be explored in chapter 4). The aim of writing and distributing the testimonies, such as this one of Abraham in the Old Testament, was to stimulate faith and obedience (as will be discussed in chapter 5).

Who is *us*? As Christian readers of the bible, we are not only interested in the original context of the Old Testament (what it meant to *them*), but also what the text means to *us* as a Christian community. The New Testament church lies in continuity with ancient Israel. This is not because we are genetic descendants of Abraham (though that may be true for some), but descendants through the reality of faith in Jesus Christ. In asking what the text means to *us*, we are asking how Christ fulfils the Old Testament scripture. Sometimes Christ directly fulfils a promise – like that given to Abraham that through his seed all the nations of the earth would be blessed. The New Testament writers looked back to the testimony of Abraham and saw that Jesus' life and ministry was in continuity with this promise because God sent Jesus to turn us from our wicked ways (Acts 3:26) and bring us into relationship with him. He was a literal descendant of Abraham who has brought blessing to the world. But while Jesus Christ directly fulfils this promise it doesn't mean that we have to find Jesus behind every rock in the Old Testament. Instead we look for how his life and ministry can be seen in the patterns or the testimony of the bigger story.

Likewise as part of the church, we also are in continuity with Jesus Christ and the faith of ancient Israel. So we can also ask how we (as part of the Christian community) fulfil this passage. As God gave the promise of blessing to Abraham that was not only significant to the ancient Israelite community but fulfilled in Christ, we continue this promise as part of the Christian community. Although Christ is the promised seed and fulfilment of Abraham's promise, it doesn't end there. According to Galatians, we are also the continuation of this promise (Galatians 3:14). As we take this blessing of the good news to the nations, so we also become the means of blessing. This passage in Genesis 12 is significant to *us* as we become the 'blessing' by bringing the good news of the ultimate blessing of Jesus Christ. This mandate for missions can be seen as a continuation of the older covenant testimony of Abraham. Further description of this question of the significance of the text for *us* is given in chapter 6.

Who is *me*? When you read the bible, you read it for all sorts of reasons, as we noted above. So each reader needs to ask: what is the significance of this passage for *me*? By asking this question, we are inviting God to speak into our lives through the words of the bible. So this question addresses the meaningfulness and message of the biblical text to you as the individual reader. What is God saying to you personally through this passage? What appeals to you from this passage that is specific to your life and unique to where you're at right now? We call this the illumination of the biblical text by the Holy Spirit. It is like a light has turned on inside. So it is important that you read the Old Testament with an open heart and mind, and trust the Holy Spirit to speak directly from the text of Scripture into your own life. This is in addition to reflecting on the significance of the passage in its own time (for *them*). The biblical text might then be challenging you to a new way of living or thinking. So as you read the Old Testament, you can anticipate and expect God to speak to you through its pages. You can allow the bible to transform your mind and life. How you can do this is further explained in chapter 7. But it's important that in doing this step that you also ask the two previous questions. As you search the text for your own life, it is crucial that you also keep in mind what the text means to 'them' and 'us'.

With these tools we can uncover a wealth of richness when reading the Old Testament – to discover who our God is …how God acts… and how we can reflect this magnificent God in our lives and community. But that is not all! Once we have been equipped with these strategic questions, we can begin to apply *them, us & me* to the biblical text in Part II. We do this by examining the major events in the testimony of ancient Israel (as presented in the Old Testament). As we explore this general testimony, we can ask these three questions to the events, concepts and some specific passages of the Old Testament. But what is this testimony?

The testimony of ancient Israel as presented in the Old Testament began at creation with humanity being the special act of God's deliberate work. It then centred on one family, led by Abraham, and his descendants who dwelt in an area known as the Fertile Crescent. This family continued to be blessed and multiplied.

However in a time of famine they moved to Egypt. After a while the Egyptians feared the expanding numbers of this family group, so they made Abraham's descendants become slaves. But these slaves cried out to God in this time of crisis. God heard their cry and acted because of the promise he had made with Abraham and his descendants. God sent a deliverer, Moses, and through him miraculously liberated the people so they could worship him.[1] Once liberated from Egypt they entered into covenant with God, and became a nation under God. They became known as God's people: called God's 'son'. At this time they were given instructions in relating to God and one another (law); instructions in worship (sacrificial system) and the construction of the place of worship (tabernacle).

While the ancient Israelites were called out of Egypt to resettle in the 'Promised Land', the first generation of ex-slaves responded in fear, rather than faith. As a result, they did not immediately enter the land of promise. Instead they experienced the wilderness wanderings for forty years. Before they entered the land, Moses gave instructions for the next generation in the law and covenant (outlined in the book of Deuteronomy) which they re-affirmed. Moses also instructed them on how to live successfully in the land. The next generation under the leadership of Joshua entered the Promised Land.

The ancient Israelites settled in the land of promise (in the Fertile Crescent) and were led by judges through an unstable period. Eventually under their first stable king, David, they established their kingdom. However it soon cracked and the kingdom divided into the north (Israel) and the south (Judah). This was followed by a long cycle of turning away from God and then back to him. Yet ancient Israel were not the only people around at this time. There were other larger nations right next door. Being small fish in a big pond of the ancient Near East, the two kingdoms got caught up in the wider political problems and conflict. Eventually due to their rejection of God the two kingdoms collapsed. First the northern kingdom was captured by Assyria. Later, the southern kingdom was captured by Babylon and taken into exile. Interestingly while the southern kingdom (Judah) was in captivity, the Babylonians were overthrown by the Persians. After a period of time, the Persians allowed the Judeans (or Jews as they were then known) to return to their homeland to rebuild the city and Temple. They introduced many religious and social reforms but always struggled in their identity and thirst for political independence.

This epic testimony is not simple. It involves an understanding of international politics, concepts such as 'covenant' and the world-view of ancient Israel. But that is not the end of the story – as the New Testament reminds us. In the fullness of time, God sent his son (Gal 4:4) to save Israel and the nations from the cycle of sin. Christ, called Immanuel, is the ultimate evidence of 'God with us' and God for us. Where Israel failed, Jesus succeeded. Israel (like most of us) failed in their obedience. Jesus triumphed as the obedient 'son' and through his ultimate sacrifice on the cross he completes the testimony of ancient Israel's worship. He has made a new way for us to be in relationship with God. This history of God's grace and salvation shows us how God's promises are trustworthy. This testimony reminds us that God's word cannot be defeated. Even through enormous obstacles, God's word and promises prevail.

So once you have been equipped with the tools of *them, us & me* and have practiced asking these strategic questions of the Old Testament, you can begin to apply these in your regular reading and study of the bible. Knowing the right questions and right (overall) context will give you confidence in reading. That means you now don't have to skip through those difficult passages! Instead you can take the time to read, digest and value them. Through this, I hope that you will grow to love and treasure the Old Testament even more. The more you read the more it will deepen your appreciation of its contribution to our theology and daily lives.

But this method of reading the bible is not just for your own benefit. The second question – the significance of the text for *us*, the Christian community, reminds us that we do not read the bible in isolation. We are part of a wider community. This community of Christians is called the church. There is the global expression of this group, referred to as the 'church'. This is all Christians. Then there is the local expression, such as your local congregation, which is called the 'Church'. Our reading and understanding of the bible contributes to this community. God speaks to each one of us, and we can encourage others by sharing our own insights from reading the Old Testament. To express this in an appropriate way, there are group discussion questions at the end of each chapter that you can use in a small group or bible study setting. These questions are there to help stimulate and facilitate discussion.

HOW TO READ...

Once we are equipped with these tools and begin to dig for the gold in the Old Testament there are a few further considerations. It is important that when we sit down to read the bible, we do so thoughtfully and intentionally. Reading with thoughtfulness is not dissecting the bible like a science experiment. This type of reading can actually be counter-productive because we do not read it to understand, but to judge. Now this does not mean that analysing a text is not important, but when we seek *only* to gather information and not to understand or apply it, we are only half-reading. In the same way, when we read only to find significance for ourselves or read devotionally without seeking to understand, we are also only half-reading. Instead, reading thoughtfully should be more like gazing at a loved one. You appreciate and absorb the details. For example, I have three nephews and a niece. When each of these treasured children were born into our family we examined all of their little features. We studied them. We checked that they had five fingers on each hand and five toes on each foot. This examination was not to itemise the information or to perhaps criticise how red and wrinkly their newborn skin may have looked under the fluorescent lights! It was a study of concern and care for these babies. However, neither did we leave our brains at home – we began to note evidence of their unique little personalities and speculate on which parent they would most look like. Would they have dark hair or light hair? Were they giggly or serious? We reflected and pondered on what we observed. Many years later, these children have grown to confirm, and sometimes completely contradict these earlier speculations. But we have continued to cherish each child and appreciate their developing personalities as we observe and share life together. Likewise reading the bible should involve both our hearts and mind.

This also reminds us that reading the bible is a journey. I don't know about you, but I tend to be a destination person. I love that sense of completion and finality. Once when I was hiking the Milford Track in New Zealand, my friend Hilary commented on our first day: "Please slow down or we will finish this 4 day hike by lunch time!". Forget looking at the beautiful scenery, magnificent waterfalls and inquisitive wildlife, I wanted to get to the end. I wanted to reach the destination. Sometimes we can read the bible in this way. We are so keen to finish reading our allocated chapter for the day that we race through it. Then once at the end we aren't really sure of what we just read! By rushing and being destination-orientated, we do not absorb what the text is saying. Sure, we might have a general grasp of what it was about, but we have missed the subtleties and details of the passage.

Sometimes this hurried reading is actually a symptom of fear. This is especially true of reading the Old Testament. We may not have understood a passage or be fearful that we will read something that unsettles us or even contradicts our current knowledge of God. So we panic and race through the text until we find something that we *do* understand and ignore the rest. Of course, I cannot guarantee that you will understand or even value everything that you read. In fact, what I can guarantee is that if you read the Old Testament thoughtfully, you will discover some unsettling passages! The Old Testament describes some experiences and events that are considered horrific and barbaric in our contemporary society, such as the mass genocide of the Canaanites in Joshua or the sacrifice of Jephthah's daughter in one of the darkest times in ancient Israel's history (Judges 10-11).[2] Sometimes we do not know what to *do* with these texts. This is further intensified by the fact that the biblical narratives often just report events without commenting on whether they were right or wrong. We will discuss this further in chapter 5. Or sometimes, we read texts that seem to portray God in a way that is different to our knowledge up to that point. This can also be uncomfortable. But reading the bible is not about simply reinforcing our own ideas or presuppositions. Sometimes our theology will be challenged, and reading the bible intentionally requires us to be willing to adjust our views if the data or text requires us to re-think them. But as we read the bible thoughtfully and utilise the tools of the trade outlined in this book, they can set us well on the way to understanding. They can also help to give us confidence.

Of course, no matter how amazing I think this book is, it would be remiss of me to let you think that this is the only resource available to assist you in reading and understanding the Old Testament. There are many other excellent introductory books, commentaries and topical books available through Christian book suppliers that I encourage you to make use of. For example, if you are seriously challenged by the ethical dilemmas of mass genocide in Joshua, then there are commentaries and topical books to help you wrestle with the particularities of this issue (see chapter 14). Another equally important resource to help you understand the bible better is your local church community. It is in this place of security and community that you should be able to share your concerns, doubts, fears or hopes from the bible. By sharing your thoughts at an appropriate time in an open and supportive discussion with your friends or leader, you can help each other in this simple yet difficult task of reading the bible. You might even discover that you are not alone or that someone has already journeyed through an area of doubt before you. This reminds us that each of us contribute to the wealth of understanding within our communities. We are on this journey together.

However, of all these resources, I think that the best help available for us is the Holy Spirit. Although this will be discussed in chapter 7 it is important to note here that one of the roles of the Holy Spirit is to guide us into truth (John 16:12). When we read the text with an ear to what the Holy Spirit is saying, we are privy to some amazing insights! This illumination of the Holy Spirit is sometimes called an 'aha' moment – when we really 'get' it. It's like the comprehension has dropped into our hearts and minds. This doesn't mean that the Holy Spirit doesn't work through our minds or the study process. The Holy Spirit works by illuminating a truth which comes from our reading or study of the bible. Sometimes though we are unsure if what we are hearing is the Holy Spirit, ourselves, or another source. We must always be willing to test this 'revelation' by submitting it to the consideration of the wider community and our broader knowledge of Scripture. For this reason, when we utilise all three of these resources (of the Holy Spirit, community and Scripture) we are on a winning path! But the journey has just begun. Let's learn more about the uniqueness of the Old Testament and how we got this bible that is so important to us.

Group Discussion Questions:

1. Describe the tools for reading the Old Testament outlined in this chapter.

2. In your group, write a brief timeline of the main events in the history of ancient Israel.

3. Can you apply the 3 tools (or questions of *them, us & me*) to read a specific passage? Without looking at the notes, try discussing how you might apply the tools to Genesis 12:1-3.

4. How effective are these tools for you? What do you need to do to improve your use of them?

Recommended Reading

⸙ Fee, Gordon D., & Stuart, Douglas, *How to Read the Bible For all its Worth*, 3rd Ed., (Grand Rapids: Zondervan, 2003).

This is almost the third testament for many Christian readers of the bible. It outlines in a practical way the different genres or types of writing found in the bible and how to read those forms appropriately.

⸙ LaSor, William S., Hubbard, David A. & Bush, Frederic W., *Old Testament Survey: The Message, Form, and Background of the Old Testament*, 2nd Ed., (Grand Rapids: Eerdmans Press, 1996).

This is an excellent introductory book for the student and general reader. It introduces and describes each book of the Old Testament while also presenting some vital background information on its formation.

⸙ Birch, Bruce C., Brueggemann, Walter, Fretheim, Terrence E., & Petersen, David L., *A Theological Introduction to the Old Testament*, 2nd Ed., (Nashville: Abingdon Press, 2005).

For the more serious student, this introductory book covers all the bases. It addresses technical and critical issues in a beautifully written volume.

Endnotes:

1. Although the masculine pronoun will be used to refer to God, this in no way implies that God is only defined by the masculine gender. God transcends all gender categories, but has revealed himself throughout history to us in categories we can understand, such as father, mother, shepherd, etc.

2. LaSor et al, notes in chapter 10 of the book, *Old Testament Survey: The Message, Form, and Background of the Old Testament*, 2nd Ed., (Grand Rapids: Eerdmans, 1996) that the idea that God could command the complete extermination of a people group seems offensive. While some scholars have suggested that this God of the Conquest is not the same as the God of the New Testament (see the discussion on Marcion in the next chapter), this is not true to the overall witness of the Bible that sees continuity in the witness of God in both Testaments. The response of LaSor to this ethical dilemma is to note that this was common practice of the day. This does not make the practice right or appropriate for today, but helps to recognise it was a different culture, time and place. Yet LaSor also notes that the actual reasoning for the extermination of the Canaanites is for the protection of the faith of the ancient Israelites so that they would not be contaminated by the evil practices of Canaan. This issue will be discussed more in chapter 14. However, to read further discussion on these texts from a theological and more scholarly reading on both the Joshua and Judges texts see Birch, B.C., Brueggemann, W., Fretheim, T.E., & Petersen, D.L., *A Theological Introduction to the Old Testament*, 2nd Ed., (Nashville: Abingdon, 2005), chapter 6. A thematic approach to the concept of God as a Warrior is offered in Longman, T. & Reid, D.G., *God is warrior*, (Zondervan, 1995). A contrasting view is offered by Regina Schwartz in *The Curse of Cain: The Violent Legacy of Monotheism*, (Chicago: Chicago University Press, 1997).

Chapter 2

WHAT IS THE OLD TESTAMENT?

When we first begin to read the Old Testament, one of the first things that strike us is that it is not a cohesive book. Well, it is not like reading a Jane Austen or a Tolkien novel. Instead, it's more like reading an anthology (a collection of different writings). It has common themes rather than a single storyline. In fact, you just have to look up the contents page to see that it comprises 39 individual 'books' of all different weird and wonderful titles. Just trying to pronounce some of these names can cause us to break into a sweat. Actually the word 'bible' comes from the Greek language to mean "the books". This leads us to ask: What is so special about these books? What actually is the Old Testament? On one level, this question is easy. It's the first half of the Christian bible. It is the part of Scripture before the coming of Christ. But what actually is it? Where did it come from? What is so important about these scrolls written in ancient Hebrew and some Aramaic? This is when the questions start to get a bit tricky. However, these questions are vital for us to consider if we are going to be confident readers of Scripture, and understand what we are reading.

There are three different pictures or analogies that we can use to understand what the bible is, and how we got it. Firstly, the bible is like a map.[1] It provides guidance and direction for our lives written by someone who has already been through the terrain we are travelling. But as anyone trying to find an unfamiliar place on a street directory has discovered, reading maps aren't always obvious. They require us to read them the right way if we are going to arrive at the right place. A second analogy to help us understand the nature of these inspired writings is the Old Testament as a collection of testimonies.[2] The 39 books of the Old Testament are like 39 different testimonies that give witness to the actions of God in the world. By listening to these testimonies that have been collected over hundreds of years, we can learn about God, ourselves and this world that God has created. Finally, we can understand the bible as a measuring stick.[3] It provides the standard by which we measure all our theology and revelation of God. Studying and understanding the nature of the Old Testament and how we got it, gives us insight into the workings of God. The bible is the product of the activity of both people and God. The result is this treasure chest and record of God's activity in history to continue to guide, encourage and inspire us. When we read the Old Testament using the tools outlined in this book, we can lift the lid on this treasure chest and discover the gold.

THE OLD TESTAMENT AS A MAP

As you may have noticed, one of my favourite hobbies is hiking. I love the feeling of getting away from everything with some kindred nature lovers and just absorbing the beauty of God's creation. I inherited this love from my dad who always took (or sometimes dragged!) our family camping. While on a hike, there are usually plenty of signposts along the track. However it is always crucial to take a map. The map provides the detail needed to keep us on track. On longer hikes, the map can mean the difference between being lost or found. Recently I was on a long hike in Tasmania with some good friends across the Cradle Mountain National Park. One of our friends, Ann-Marie, was a local and experienced hiker, so she was our guide for the seven days and the guardian of the map. On the fifth day we needed to split into two groups, so Ann-Marie gave us instructions while she went with the map and the second group. I was in the first group that were happily hiking through the beautiful bushland but suddenly reached an unexpected intersection. We had a choice of two paths. Which path were we meant to take? We remembered Ann-Marie's instructions, but without the map we were unsure. We had to make a decision without adequate information. We needed the map to guide us. I wish I could say that we prayed and a light fell on the right pathway, but that did not happen. Instead we took what seemed to be the most obvious track only to discover several kilometres later that it was the wrong way and had to re-trace our steps. Our backpacks seemed extra heavy on that return trip. We needed a map!

When we think of our Christian life as a journey, we see that the bible is like a map. Throughout this journey we travel through various terrains of 'ups' and 'downs'. The bible is the map that guides us and directs us along the path. While you can study a map from the outside to gain information about the terrain, it is not until you are actually living in and exploring the territory as a local that the map makes sense.[4] As we read the map, we discover a lot about ourselves, about the journey of salvation and about God (the map-maker). We are required to walk according to the directions on the map. If we don't we will get lost, hurt or go round in circles! As we travel along this right path we are transformed through the process of the journey. Reading the bible transforms us into new people. As renewed people, we eventually reach our destination. If you are looking for guidance for your life, the bible can be a map to help direct you.

But anyone that has tried to read a map knows that they are not always easy to read. Maps require interpretation. Maps can be read the wrong way. They can be misinterpreted. While the tools outlined in this book can give you the skills required to read the 'map' (i.e. Old Testament), reading the bible is not just an individual exercise. When I first began to learn to read maps and use a compass, my dad always checked what I thought was a 'sure thing'. Sometimes I had us on the right track, sometimes I didn't. A local church community similarly provides guidance for its members in reading the 'map' of the bible skilfully. As you begin to learn to read the Old Testament with the tools provided, you can share and 'check' what you have discovered with others. In this way, the community acts as a safeguard. Just like hiking and map-reading, understanding the bible is not meant to be a solo enterprise. This leads us to the second analogy.

The Old Testament as a collection of testimonies

Reading the Old Testament is about hearing the testimony of people of faith who have gone before you. It is listening and understanding their stories and experiences. It is learning from their successes and mistakes. It is about seeing how God has worked in the past through their lives. By hearing their stories we can gain insight into how God can work in our life. Once you have heard their testimony for its insight and encouragement, you can begin to work out how their message applies to your life. This will be different from *them*, because they are not you. For starters, they lived in a different culture and time in history. But still they have an amazing message for you to learn from.

The various testimonies of the Old Testament include stories about God speaking and calling an individual like Abraham (Genesis 12). The testimonies include poems about feeling abandoned but then remembering and trusting in God's unfailing love (Psalm 13). They also include practical wisdom for our journey through life (Proverbs 1). It is significant to note that these testimonies are presented in various different types of writing (that will be discussed in chapter 5). They were also written at various times - they didn't just fall from heaven in a ready-made volume. There is incredible diversity in the Old Testament as God acted and spoke in many different ways throughout the history of ancient Israel. Sometimes these testimonies emphasise different and seemingly contradictory aspects of God. Yet despite this diversity of witness, there is also a unity to the Old Testament as it points to the one God. These testimonies are about God at work – God speaking, acting, guiding, judging and loving. It is the testimony of ancient Israel as they witness to God's action and intervention in their own story. We don't know what God was doing in Rome, New York, Beijing or Sydney at that time because this is the testimony of ancient Israel.

Understanding the Old Testament in this way can help us to appreciate why it is a collection of 39 books, and not just one really long story. It developed over a long period of time. The Old Testament also has a lengthy history. Each of these testimonies were treasured by the ancient community. They were told, re-told and passed on to each new generation. This emphasises that their society was non-literate. The common person couldn't read or write books so the testimonies were passed on through an oral tradition. They were eventually written down over a period of approximately 1,000 years (1400-400 BC). These testimonies come to us through centuries of collecting, editing, copying, and translating. For many of the books, we're not even fully sure when they were first written. But they have been preserved and recognised as 'tried and true' by the ancient Israelite community and tradition. While there are many detailed studies of how these oral traditions were passed on and how they came to be written down, for the purposes of this study, we will just deal with the bible that we have in our hands.[5] What we do know for sure is that around the time of the exile (after 587BCE), the Pentateuch was established as a unique section known as Torah ('law'). The rest of what was in this Old Testament (or Hebrew bible as it is referred to by Jewish readers) was not established until around 100 years before the coming of Christ. Even at this point the actual order of the books (apart from the Torah) was very fluid and debated even several hundreds of years after Christ.

While the bible is unique, it still does have striking similarities with the writings of other people groups in the ancient world. This recognises that while ultimately the bible is a gift from God, it was given to a community in a particular place, time and culture. This community of the Old Testament were living in the Middle Eastern area hundreds and hundreds of years before the time of Christ and the Roman Empire. They spoke a Semitic language known as Hebrew along with some Aramaic (the trade language of the time). These are the two original languages of the Old Testament. Both are Semitic languages (a word derived from the name of Noah's son Shem). They are languages with a common origin.[6] Hebrew appears to be a Canaanite dialect adopted by Abraham's family when they settled in Canaan (Isaiah 19:18) and continued as the spoken language of Palestine (Canaan) until the time of the exile. After that, Aramaic became the main language spoken by the people. It had been the official language of diplomacy and commerce under the Assyrian empire (8th century). Both Ezra and Daniel contain lengthy passages in Aramaic. Aramaic was quite likely the native tongue of Jesus and most New Testament authors. However the majority of the Old Testament is written in Hebrew. What we read is a translation from the original language. Many of those tongue-twisting names in the Old Testament are a direct translation from the Hebrew. Just trying to read some of these names (my personal favourite is "Maher-Shalal-Hash-Baz" in Isaiah 8:1) highlights that their language and world was very different to ours. Yet, the bible also comes from God. Each of the writers living in their place, time and culture were inspired by God. Their writings reflect the hand of God on their lives and thoughts. Therefore it has the touch of both God and people. This should not surprise us but actually remind us of another truth in the bible: Jesus Christ.

As Christians, we affirm that Jesus Christ is both God and human. This does not mean that he is half-God and half-human, but fully both. While Jesus was on the earth he lived in a particular time and place, he spoke the language of his earthly family and followed the customs of the community into which he was born. This same way of thinking about Jesus Christ can help us to understand the bible. The bible is both a divine and a human book.[7] It didn't just drop out of the sky and into the lap of the biblical writers, but developed out of the language, culture, history and experiences of the ancient Israelites. I actually find this thought comforting because it reminds me that God speaks to each of us where we are at. Wherever we are, whatever language we speak, whenever we call, God will speak to us in a relevant way using our language and culture and time. As God spoke to the ancient Israelites in their language, God will speak to me. God demonstrates this eagerness and desire to communicate and fellowship with us no matter what it takes. God will graciously meet us where we are at.

Yet while God speaks to us where we are at, it is important to recognise that we are not ancient Israelites. I hope this doesn't come as a shock to you! But there is a gap between now and then. We live in a very different culture and time. This is a part of the difficulty of reading the Old Testament. We are separated from the culture and time of Old Testament by thousands of years. So we can't just 'cut and paste' ancient cultural norms onto our contemporary setting because times have changed. If I have mould in my bathroom I don't have to call the priest to see if I should remove the contaminated tiles (Leviticus 14: 33-53)! But even so, we can learn important principles from their testimony.

This collection of testimonies belonged firstly to the ancient Israelite community. This includes the religion and people out of which Judaism later developed. So the testimonies belong to Judaism as well. But from this group of ancient Israelite people, Jesus Christ was born. This is very important to the New Testament writers, and is the very first thing that the first book, Matthew, tells us. Jesus Christ is part of the family of the Old Testament. The followers of Jesus (later called Christians) also developed out of this community of Judaism to become quite a recognisable and separate group. This community of Christians not only treasured the writings of the ancient Israelites (Old Testament) but included some of the writings of their own community called the New Testament. Because I am a Christian reader, I refer to it as the 'Old Testament' even though I recognise that it has a different name and order in Judaism (which I will discuss below). Now the terms 'Old' and 'New' don't mean that the one is rusty and worn while the other is fresh. It refers to the term 'testamentum' (Latin) which means "covenant". This is a pledge or promise – a concept discussed in chapter 9. So the Old Testament is the agreement made between God and the ancient Israelites. The Old Testament is the older covenant before the coming of Christ while the New Testament is the newer covenant that was begun by the life and ministry of Jesus Christ. As Christians, we stand in continuity with this faith of ancient Israel.

However the adoption of writings from ancient Israel has been questioned in various historic times. In the early second century, a scholar named Marcion argued that the God of the Old Testament was incompatible with the God of the New Testament. He argued for the removal of the Old Testament from the treasured writings of the church. This forced the early believers to really think about and seek God as to what should and shouldn't be included in the Christian Bible. Eventually, they concluded with hearty assent that the Old Testament was consistent with the New Testament. While this view of Marcion was overturned by the early Church councils, sometimes we still practice his beliefs when we ignore or reject parts of the Old Testament we don't understand. For example, we practice Marcionism when we construct the Old Testament as a caricature of the negative law while making the New Testament as a paragon of positive grace. This ignores the grace of God in creation, in redemption at the exodus, in the giving of the law, and in God's continued faithfulness. The God of ancient Israel that the Old Testament witnesses to is the same God incarnate in Jesus Christ. This leads us to the third analogy.

BIBLE AS A MEASURING STICK

The contents of the bible are referred to as a 'canon'. This does not mean it is a piece of military equipment, but comes from an Akkadian word (via the Hebrew and Greek languages) which means "measuring rod".[8] It is something used to give a straight line. By understanding the bible as a measuring stick, we recognise that it sets the standard for our faith, experience and doctrine. The bible does not *just* provide testimonies that describe the knowledge and experience of God. As contemporary readers of the bible, it becomes the judge and corrector of our experience and knowledge of God. This is particularly important in faith traditions, such as Pentecostal, Charismatic or Methodist communities where the experience of God is emphasised.[9] It is the authority or straight line that we measure everything from. The Christian "canon" comprises the Old Testament and the New Testament. As noted above, Christians inherited their canon from Judaism. Their writings gave us the Old Testament. We read the same books as the followers of Judaism. Christians then added the teachings of Christ and writings from the early church to make the New Testament. From that time onwards there developed different versions of the Old Testament with different order and arrangements. So how were the books of the Old Testament arranged?

If you look at the contents page of your Old Testament, you will notice that the books are arranged in a set order. But this order is not the same for all faith traditions that utilise the books of the Old Testament. Recently I moved house, and one of the things I had to do was to pack up all the books on my bookshelf and put them into boxes. Once moved, I had to then unpack all the books and arrange them on the bookshelves once again. But as I was re-shelving them, I realised that I had quite a few options of how I was going to arrange them. If I wanted to be artistic, I could put them on the shelf according to their size. Like the books in the section of the 'Minor Prophets', I could arrange them from the biggest books to the smallest. If I wanted to be practical, I could have arranged all my books according to their type of writing – all the novels would go together separate from the cookbooks. This is a bit like how we have the poetry and wisdom writings together separate from the Prophets. Or if I wanted to follow the development of ideas, I could put them in some kind of order of chronology - so the novels begin with earlier literature and then progress in order through the classics

Figure 1.0: *Comparative Table of Old Testament Books in the canons of the Protestant, Catholic and Hebrew Bibles.*

Protestant	Catholic	TaNaK
Genesis	Genesis	Genesis
Exodus	Exodus	Exodus
Leviticus	Leviticus	Leviticus
Numbers	Numbers	Numbers
Deuteronomy	Deuteronomy	Deuteronomy
Joshua	Joshua	Joshua
Judges	Judges	Judges
Ruth	Ruth	Samuel (includes full text)
1 Samuel	1 Samuel	Kings (includes full text)
2 Samuel	2 Samuel	Isaiah
1 Kings	1 Kings	Jeremiah
2 Kings	2 Kings	Ezekiel
1 Chronicles	1 Chronicles	Hosea
2 Chronicles	2 Chronicles	Joel
Ezra	Ezra	Amos
Nehemiah	Nehemiah	Obadiah
Esther	Tobit (Greek)	Jonah
Job	Judith (Greek)	Micah
Psalms	Esther	Nahum
Proverbs	Job	Habakkuk
Ecclesiastes	Psalms	Zephaniah
Song of Solomon	Proverbs	Haggai
Isaiah	Ecclesiastes	Zechariah
Jeremiah	Song of Solomon	Malachi
Lamentations	Wisdom of Solomon (Greek)	Psalms
Ezekiel	Ecclesiasticus (Greek)	Job
Daniel	Isaiah	Proverbs
Hosea	Jeremiah	Ruth
Joel	Lamentations	Song of Songs
Amos	Baruch (Greek)	Ecclesiastes
Obadiah	Ezekiel	Lamentations
Jonah	Daniel	Esther
Micah	Hosea	Daniel
Nahum	Joel	Ezra
Habakkuk	Amos	Nehemiah
Zephaniah	Obadiah	Chronicles (inc. full text)
Haggai	Jonah	
Zechariah	Micah	
Malachi	Nahum, Habakkuk, Zephaniah, Haggai, Zechariah, Malachi	
	1 & 2 Maccabees	

to contemporary fiction. This would be like how the 'historical' books (Former Prophets) are arranged. So when it came to arranging the Old Testament, all of these types of methods were used.[10]

There are three main versions or arrangements of the Old Testament. These are the canons of the Hebrew Bible (used in Judaism), the Catholic Bible and the Protestant Bible (see Figure 1.0). The Hebrew Bible is organised into three distinct sections. Commonly called the TaNaK, it is an acronym made up of the initial consonants of the three major divisions of the Hebrew Bible: *Torah* ('Law'), the *Nebi'im* ('Prophets'), and the *Kethubim* ('Writings'). The Hebrew Bible recognises only the books written in the Hebrew language. This same rationale was adopted in the formation of the Protestant Bible.

The Torah refers to the first five books: Genesis, Exodus, Leviticus, Numbers and Deuteronomy. These were traditionally called the 'Five books of Moses' (also known as the 'Pentateuch'). This section of literature is considered to have the highest scriptural authority in the Jewish tradition. It is arranged developmentally. Its order represents the chronology of the testimony it describes from creation to the exodus to the death of Moses, just before the Israelites entered the Promised Land.

The Prophets are actually divided into two groups. The *former* prophets include Joshua, Judges, Samuel and Kings. These are what we sometimes refer to as the historical books. They are arranged developmentally to represent the chronology of the testimony it describes. It journeys through events such as the entrance to the Promised Land to the defeat of the northern kingdom and eventual exile of the southern kingdom, Judah. The *latter* prophets are Isaiah, Jeremiah, Ezekiel, and the twelve Minor Prophets (these are one scroll). These were the words of the prophets of ancient Israel. This section probably reached its final form by the second century BCE. It has generally considered in Judaism to have a lesser authority than the Torah. Unlike the previous sections, the latter prophets are arranged aesthetically – from the biggest book Isaiah to the smallest book Malachi.

The third section of the Tanak is the Writings. This section is made up of a miscellaneous collection of eleven books. It contains the three great poetry books of Psalms, Job and Proverbs. It is also made up of the "Five Scrolls" of Ruth, Song of Songs, Ecclesiastes, Lamentations and Esther. This is followed by the seemingly random placement at the end of the apocalyptic book of Daniel and historical books of Ezra-Nehemiah, and Chronicles. While these books were recognised as part of the canon before the coming of Christ, they were only really put in this order well into the Christian era. They were also considered to have less authority than the Torah or Prophets. While I've classified these books as being more randomly placed, their ordering is still very significant. Their arrangement is quite different to the order of books in the Christian versions (Catholic and Protestant Bibles).[11]

The order of the Christian Bible was greatly influenced by one of the church fathers Athanasius. He placed the Prophets after the Writings to bring them closer to the New Testament so that the Old Testament ends with the Prophets, specifically Malachi. In comparison, the Hebrew Bible ends with Chronicles. Why are they arranged differently? It primarily represents the different theology and interests of the groups. The Christian Bible points to the coming Messiah (fulfilled in Christ). The Christian Bible places the Prophetic books at the end to pave the way for the New Testament as the fulfilment of the Old Testament prophecies. This emphasises the New Testament as a prophetic continuation of the Old Testament, rather than a historical continuation of the nation of Israel. As Christians, we continue the testimony of the Old Testament. However we continue it as people of faith, not as people belonging to the geographic, political nation of Israel. In comparison, the Hebrew Bible looks to the fulfilment of the patriarchal promises for land. Chronicles is an attempt to explain the reasons for the exile and reflects the importance of land to the Jewish community. It finishes with the people outside of the Promised Land, longing to return to the land.

While the order reflects the different emphases of theology, does it really matter? Does the order effect how we interpret the books? Let's consider this for a moment. I have had the privilege of preaching and teaching the Old Testament in Italy. The Italian people are extremely hospitable and love to share their rich culinary delights. While I was at a house in Sicily, the host served some antipasto of rockmelon wrapped in *prosciutto* (a special ham). It sounds a bit weird but it was delicious. The sweetness of the melon softened the salted ham to create an explosive contradiction of taste. Then at the end of the meal, they served more rockmelon again. This time they served it with some cake. When I had the melon with the cake, it tasted completely different to when I ate it with ham – much more sweet and sugary. What I ate with the melon affected its taste. In the same way, when we change the order of the Old Testament books it similarly changes their 'taste'.

For example, where is the book of Ruth located in the Christian Bible? It's after the book of Judges and before Samuel. What taste does it have? This placement emphasises its historical location during the chaotic time of the Judges and serves to introduce the origins of David. This David became the greatest King of Israel. He was the messiah, the one anointed for the task of kingship. From this lineage of David, the ultimate messiah – Jesus Christ – would come. That's the 'taste' the arrangement of Ruth in the Christian Bible. Through this order, we can savour the flavour of the 'salt' of Jesus Christ on our lips. It is a flavour to relish!

However, where is the book of Ruth located in the Hebrew Bible? The book comes after Proverbs and before Song of Songs. Proverbs ends with a summary in chapter 31 of what wisdom looks like in the example of the 'woman of valour'. The Proverbs 31 woman is an amazing example of wisdom in action. That same term ('woman of valour') is used by Boaz to describe Ruth. So in this placement, Ruth also becomes an example of wisdom in action. She is the embodiment of the Proverbs 31 woman. It emphasises the necessity of wisdom in the choices and responsibilities in life. And by reading it before the love poetry of Song of Songs, it highlights the eventual triumph of life and love. It leaves the 'taste' of love's sweetness on our lips. So the order of these books has theological implications and actually impacts what we get out of our reading.

But this is not where the differences end. You may have also noticed that some Old Testament canons have additional books. While the Hebrew canon comprises the same books as the Protestant Old Testament (though in a different order), the Catholic version has some extra books. These were included in the Septuagint (or the LXX). The Septuagint is the Greek translation of the Old Testament dating from the second century BCE. It includes the books of Maccabees, Judith and the Wisdom of Solomon. The Catholic Bible refers to these as 'deutero-canonical' books. Protestants refer to them as 'apocryphal' (or hidden) books, and exclude them from their Old Testament. While the apocryphal books were valued by Jews they were not regarded as having authority equal to the books of the Hebrew canon. This reflects a rift in the history of the church from about the fourth century between the Eastern and Western church. The Western church allowed these extra books, while the church in the East kept to the stricter Hebrew canon. During the Protestant Reformation, the reformers chose to also use this stricter Hebrew canon. So for the Protestant church, the apocryphal books are valued but not regarded as having authority equal to the books of the Hebrew canon.

From this brief study of the 'canon' we can appreciate the history and development of the Old Testament. It is from this understanding of *what* the Old Testament is that we can begin to explore *how* to read it in more detail. However, just a note before we move onto the method of reading. People often ask me which translation of the bible is the best one to study. Unfortunately there is no *one* best translation. Each version that we use is exactly that – a translation. This is important to remember before we commit ourselves to dying on the hill of what our 'bible says'. In general, our English Bible translations tend to follow one of two basic approaches (although with varying levels of consistency). They either follow a formal correspondence or a dynamic equivalence. A translation that has a formal correspondence will try and stay as close as possible to the original language in both vocabulary and sentence structure. This is positive in that it corresponds closely to the original, but often means it is difficult to read because Hebrew is very different to English! This sometimes makes it awkward and stilted, and in this sense may not be like the original in flow. Translations that utilise this approach include the 'NASB', 'EV' and 'NKJV' versions. On the other hand, a translation that has a dynamic equivalence will try and communicate the meaning of the original text in as fluent a way as possible. But while it may capture the flow and tone, it may not represent the exact vocabulary of the original text. Translations that utilise this approach include the 'TNIV', 'NLT' and 'GNB' versions.[12] But the best way to decide which translation to use is to use both. When really digging deep into your Old Testament text, it's good to use more than one version. This way you get the flow of the idea as well as the particular words used. So now that you are armed with your English translation and an appreciation of the history of this ancient text, you are ready to beginning digging with the tools of *them, us & me.*

GROUP QUESTIONS:

1. What is the difference in the order of the books in the Hebrew, Protestant and Catholic Bibles?

2. If you could change the order of the Protestant Bible, how would you arrange it?

3. What are some of the problems (or challenges!) of choosing a bible translation?

4. Do you think the 'The Message' bible is a good or a bad translation? Why or why not?

RECOMMENDED READING

⯈ Barton, J., *How the Bible Came to Be,* (Westminster/ John Knox Press, 1998).

A solid presentation of the development of the canon, and issues in the process of canonisation.

⯈ Orr-Ewing, A., *Why Trust the Bible? Answers to 10 Tough Questions,* (Leicester: IVP, 2005).

This is a great book for all readers (particularly university readers) that emphasises the uniqueness of the bible. Rather than avoid some of the tricky questions (like the ethical dilemmas raised in the introduction of this book), it addresses and resolves the issue concisely.

ENDNOTES

1. This description of the Bible as a map is utilised by Autry in an article entitled 'Dimensions of Hermeneutics in Pentecostal Focus' (*Journal of Pentecostal Theology,* Vol 3, 1993, pp.29-50.

2. This description of the Bible as testimony is particularly developed by Walter Brueggemann in his magnus opus *Theology of the Old Testament: Testimony, Dispute, Advocacy,* (Minneapolis: Fortress, 1997).

3. This description is based on the definition of "canon", which means a 'measuring stick'.

4. Autry, A.C., 'Dimensions of Hermeneutics in Pentecostal Focus', *Journal of Pentecostal Theology,* Vol 3, 1993, p.43.

5. For a general examination of the formation and history of the Old Testament see LaSor, W.S., Hubbard, D.A. & Bush, F.W., *Old Testament Survey: The Message, Form, and Background of the Old Testament*, 2nd Ed., (Grand Rapids: Eerdmans, 1996), chapter 47: 'Formation of the Old Testament'. For an advanced study of the various processes behind the final form of the text or canon and issues relating, see Haynes & McKenzie (ed), *To Each Its Own Meaning*, Rev Ed, (Louisville: Westminster John Knox Press, 1999), chapters on 'textual', 'source' and 'form' criticisms. Also see Tov. E., *Textual Criticism of the Hebrew Bible*, (Minneapolis : Fortress Press, 1992).

6. LaSor, W.S., Hubbard, D.A. & Bush, F.W., *Old Testament Survey: The Message, Form, and Background of the Old Testament*, 2nd Ed, p.607.

7. Enns, Peter, *Inspiration and Incarnation: Evangelicals and the Problem of the Old Testament*, (Grand Rapids: Baker, 2005), p.17. Enns describes this understanding the Bible in relation to Jesus Christ as the 'Incarnational Analogy'.

8. LaSor, W.S., Hubbard, D.A. & Bush, F.W., *Old Testament Survey: The Message, Form, and Background of the Old Testament*, 2nd Ed, p.598.

9. Autry, A.C., 'Dimensions of Hermeneutics in Pentecostal Focus', p.43.

10. This analogy to describe the classification or arrangement of the Old Testament was developed by Etienne Charpentier in *How to Read the Bible: The Old and New Testaments*, (New York: Gramercy Books, 1981), p.6.

11. While the titles of the books of the Old Testament are part of the original canon, the division into chapters and verses were a much later addition. For example, Charpentier notes that the use of chapters and verse in our Bibles was devised by Stephen Langton, the Archbishop of Canterbury in 1226. See Charpentier, E., *How to Read the Bible: The Old and New Testaments*, p.6.

12. For an insightful and practical guide on how to choose a good translation, see chapter 2 of Fee, G. D., & Stuart, D., *How to Read the Bible For all its Worth*, 3rd Ed., (Grand Rapids: Zondervan, 2003).

PART I:
TOOLS TO READ

Chapter 3

Principles for reading: *THEM, US & ME*

As Christian readers of the Old Testament we identify with the characters and events of the bible. When we read about Abraham, Sarah, Moses and David, we relate to these characters. We identify with them not just because we resonate with their journeys of triumphs and failures, but because we read their story as *part of* our story. We read to know and understand their lives, but also to know and understand their lives as part of the bigger picture of what God has been doing in the world. We read it as part of our heritage of faith. As these people in the Old Testament knew God and held up the flame of God's love and rule for all to see, so we continue that task. We identify ourselves as participants in this ongoing testimony of God's story. We read the Old Testament as part of the people of God. We understand that the bible is not merely a textbook of human history, but the testimony of God's relationship with humanity. It is a history that continues up to the present community of faithful believers, and will continue in the future.

This terminology of the 'people of God' was first used in the Old Testament. In the ancient Hebrew language it was "*'am YHWH*". It is the most basic Old Testament term to describe God's special relationship to ancient Israel.[1] The Old Testament is the testimony of the first group of people to be identified by this special term of the 'people of God'. When Moses confronted Pharaoh (in the Book of Exodus), he spoke as the mouthpiece of God to let *my people* go that they may serve me (Ex 4:22-23). At the core of ancient Israel's relationship with God was the sure promise that they were the people of God (Ex 6:7; 19:3-6; Lev 26:12; Jer 11:4). This was a special relationship and therefore a unique responsibility to represent the character and nature of the God they served to the other nations adequately. While entrance to this group was exclusive to the social-political nation of ancient Israel, with the coming of Jesus Christ we see a shift. Jesus invites all people to join this 'people of God' (Matt 8:5-13). The entry requirement is not nationality but faith in Jesus Christ (1 Peter 2:9). The New Testament church lies in continuity with Israel, not as a political or social extension, but through the reality of faith.[2] The followers of Jesus have continued to invite people to join this special relationship since that time (Matt 28:18-20). As believers in Christ, we share in this history, promise and special relationship. This group called the 'people of God' has included *them* (ancient Israel), *us* (Christ and his disciples throughout the centuries) as well as *me* (and you). This does not mean that the Israelites from the time of Jesus onwards are rejected – according to the New Testament (Romans 9) they too can join this 'people of God' but the entry requirement is one of faith, not birth.

As we noted in the Introduction to this book, there are three aspects to this approach in reading Old Testament texts. These three groups (of *them*, *us* and *me*) represent the communities of faith that the Old Testament has been significant to, and whose perspective we must consider to gain the most insight in our reading. We ask: what does the text mean to *them*, to *us* and to *me*? This chapter will explore these three questions in overview. The following chapters of Part I provide more detail and examples of how these questions should be considered. What these questions highlight is that each community from the past, present and future has a unique role in the history of God's love and rule in the world. While we individually may hear God's voice or experience God intervening in our lives in some way, it does not mean we are separate from this wider story. Our lives and problems are not the centre of the universe. We are one of many participants in the history of God's rulership on the earth. As

Christians, we are participants in this kingdom. We are part of the ongoing people of God.

The approach of these three questions is a little bit like trying on different pairs of shoes. As the proverb of old says: 'walk a mile in my shoes'. This proverb encourages us to understand the lives and perspectives of other people. When we ask the significance of the Old Testament for *them* and *us*, we are trying to understand the lives and perspectives of other readers of the text. As the three questions suggests, this shoe collection contains three pairs. One pair is some old leather sandals worn by the ancient Israelite community. The second pair is a set of walking shoes worn by the expanding Christian community. The third pair is your own shoes. Wearing other people's shoes can seem a little uncomfortable at first. Our own pair seems so much more inviting. Growing up in the Blue Mountains my family had a wood fire during winter to keep us warm. I loved to snuggle up by the fire while the wind howled outside. But inevitably the wood would burn to nothing and we would need to replenish the supply from our outside stock. When it was my turn to get the wood from outside I would race to the door and put on the first pair of shoes I could find. These were usually my dad's work boots. Then I would hobble outside and grab as much wood as I could carry and stumble back inside again. Whenever I wore my dad's boots I would look at the scratches and marks on the toes and it would remind me of his hard work and toil for our family – especially in chopping all the wood for our accessible stockpile. I wasn't walking a mile in his shoes, but the brief dash to the woodpile would remind me that the world doesn't revolve around me! By walking a mile in someone else's shoes, you can appreciate their life, faith and testimony in a way that enhances your own journey.

By appreciating all three perspectives (of *them*, *us* and *me*), this approach reminds us once again that God speaks to people where they are at. Just as God spoke to the community of 'ancient Israel' in their own language, setting, culture and context with a message relevant to their situation, so God also speaks to our community. This emphasises the immanence of God – that God is close by and reaches out to us. It reminds us that scripture did not 'fall from heaven' but was the product of the historical and cultural context of the community that received it. In this sense, the bible is not trans-historical or trans-cultural. It offers a meaningful message from God to a community located in a specific historical and cultural setting. It is the same way, in essence, that we understand that God speaks to us in our own language, culture and time. So let's examine these three questions a bit more closely to see how God has spoken to people across the ages.

1. What is the significance to *them*?

When we read the Old Testament and seek to hear God's voice, we do not hear God in isolation from the testimony of the people it presents. God has not changed, and therefore the actions, character and intentions of God for humanity are the same today as they were for the biblical communities. For this reason, it is important to question the significance of the text for *them* - the people of God to whom the Old Testament text was written. More specifically, the significance for *them* refers to ancient Israel - the people and community represented in the text. You might like to think of *them* as being the ancient society before the coming of Christ in the 'old testament times'. We accept the testimony of the biblical text because it is the witness of the covenant people of God with whom we identify. While they had a long history of interaction with God, it was a dynamic community. It didn't always look exactly the same but moved from being a nomadic group to a pastoral society to a more urban group. It was a community that lived and developed over centuries. Therefore by reading commentaries and other tools, you can also discover more about the specific community a particular passage is addressing.

However this leads us to a dilemma. The problem is that this community and culture are no longer with us, so we can't know exactly how they understood the scriptures. We cannot fully retrieve their thoughts or ideas. Yet in the same way that I may not know exactly what my dad was thinking as he chopped the wood, I can get the general idea by putting on his shoes. Wearing the shoes of the ancient Israelites involves thinking about their world and culture to understand what an Old Testament passage would have meant to them. The testimony of the Old Testament is located in a specific cultural-historical period with a world-view peculiar to that time. We will never know exactly, but we can gauge a general idea by studying the context, the circumstances, the culture and what the written testimony (bible) says about the event. We listen to the testimony of *them* to discover the truth of God's past actions and character. This highlights the dual nature of testimony; there is the one who testifies and the one who hears the testimony.[3] When we read the Old Testament, we are hearing the testimony of *them*. They testify to their encounter and experience of God. Their testimony points to realities of the world. As a testimony, it points to the characteristic actions of another (namely God). The Old Testament provides us with a witness to the person and character of God. In this way, it appreciates the uniqueness of the Old Testament as a distinct testimony, (yet as part of the Christian canon that includes the New Testament). We are respecting the historical and cultural differences between their world and our world. This unknown factor is what some writers call the 'horizon' of the text.

To understand the concept of the 'horizon', picture yourself standing on a mountaintop. This is your location in history, time and culture. As you look (or read) at the Old Testament, you are looking across the horizon at another mountaintop that represents the history, time and culture of ancient Israel. What do you notice? You are not standing on the same mountain. The way you view the world, your culture is different to them. For example, while we might talk of travelling around the world or 'globe-trotting'. This speech reflects our understanding of the world as round. In contrast, the ancient Israelites seemed to view the world as a flat disc with water above and below. We view the world from different horizons. These social and cultural differences will be outlined in more detail in the next chapter. But by recognising this difference, you are acknowledging the 'horizon' of the text – the differences. But that's not where it ends.

The task of interpretation requires us to overcome the distance between the two horizons and to bridge the gap between us. So as we recognise the differences between our world and the world of 'ancient Israel', we also highlight the connections. Despite these substantial differences of time and place, there will still be similarities between people because we share a common human nature. When we read the Old Testament, we read stories of people just like us even though they lived in a different time and place. As we read, we enter their world. There will still be some similarities because God is the same and so the principles of God at work will be the same. But because God was speaking to them through their own language and culture, these principles will be presented differently. So we step back into the world of the older covenant testimony to hear their witness. But the story of God's actions in the world did not end with the ancient Israelite community. It did not end with *them*, but took a drastic new turn with the coming of Christ in the New Testament period.

2. WHAT IS THE SIGNIFICANCE TO *US*?

Through the testimony of *them*, we observe God's workings. We know and understand something of God through the record of God's dealings with ancient Israel. God has been faithful in the past, so will be faithful in the present and future. We know God to be caring for us because Psalm 23 describes the Lord as our shepherd – the very image Jesus drew upon to identify himself as God (John 10:11). For contemporary Christian readers of the bible, we are part of the 'people of God' who are different from the older covenant 'people of God'. Yet the Christian community is the continuation of God's story. This continuation is expressed through the newer covenant installed by the life and ministry of Jesus Christ. While the first question of this reading method highlights the significance of the Old Testament to *them*, the second question highlights the significance to *us*. That is, what do these words mean to the believing community of Christians? How has the life and ministry of Christ transformed how we read and understand the Old Testament?

The New Testament emphasises the salvation found only in Jesus Christ as the centre of God's actions in the world. It was the event in history that the Old Testament was moving towards. According to the New Testament writers, the Old Testament points to Jesus Christ. This is exemplified by the disciples on the road to Emmaus in Luke 24:13-9 after the resurrection of Jesus from the dead. The disciples were leaving Jerusalem in great disappointment that Jesus did not redeem Israel as they had hoped (most probably they expected political freedom for the nation). As they walked they were joined by a stranger. This man began to explain to the disciples "beginning with Moses and all the prophets" of how all the scriptures (i.e. the Old Testament) spoke of or foretold Jesus. Only later did these disciples realise that they were actually talking with Jesus himself. This approach is also a priority for Christian readers. When we read the Old Testament, we need to not only put on our sandals of the ancient Israelites, but we also need to put on the walking shoes worn by the expanding Christian community. Like the disciples on the road to Emmaus, we read the Old Testament to see how it points to Jesus Christ. We ask: what is the significance of this text for *us* as a Christian community?

We read the Old Testament to see how it points to the life and ministry of Jesus Christ. In saying this, it is important to recognise that as Christian readers we read this significance back into the Old Testament. These hints and allusions to the life and ministry of Christ were not always seen by the Old Testament writers themselves. They certainly weren't seen by the disciples on the Emmaus road. It was only after it was explained to them that they could read backwards with the eyes of their New Testament faith to see this perspective.[4] Now identifying Christ in the words of the Old Testament does not mean that we have to see Jesus foretold in every sentence. Sometimes Christ directly fulfils a promise – like that given to Abraham. Through Jesus, the seed of Abraham, all the nations of the world will be blessed. But it is important that we don't try and force it. We don't have to see Christ in every event or verse. Sometimes Christ fulfils Old Testament scripture in the patterns of the bigger story.

This is emphasised in the book of Matthew who shows how Jesus fulfils the big picture of the testimony of ancient Israel. Think back to the outline of the events of the Old Testament described in Chapter 1. A relationship with Abraham was forged and a promise from God given. From Abraham a family was born. They went down to Egypt to escape death and famine. Matthew also describes the birth of Jesus as the fulfilment of a promise. Jesus is also taken to Egypt to escape death (Matthew 2). And like ancient Israel, Jesus is called by God to leave Egypt. Like ancient Israel, Jesus goes through the waters of baptism (Matthew 3), and is identified as God's son. Then Jesus is led - like ancient Israel – into the desert wilderness for a period of 40 days. However, this is where their stories differ. It differs for a reason. The ancient Israelites prolonged their stay in the wilderness due to their faithlessness and lack of obedience (just as any of us are prone to). Eventually they left the desert behind them as they journeyed to the mountains of Moab where Moses re-delivered the law in what is called the Book of Deuteronomy. From there they were to engage in warfare to claim the Promised Land.

In contrast, Jesus demonstrates faith and emerges victorious from the wilderness to go to the mountain to re-give the law (described in Matthew 5 as the 'Beatitudes'). He also begins possession of the 'Promised Land' through healings, preaching and the exorcism of demons. However the enemies he fights are in the spiritual realm. Where ancient Israel lacked faith and behaved like an unfaithful son (like any of us would), Jesus came as the faithful son to fulfil the pattern established in the Old Testament. In this way, Jesus is the fulfilment of the Old Testament. However you may have noticed in that description that Jesus does not fulfil the testimony of ancient Israel in a literal way, like a carbon copy. There are some similarities and differences. This new covenant inaugurated by Christ as described in the New Testament text is not identical with the covenant represented in the Old Testament text, but also has differences. The question remains as to how, and how much, should Christian readers adopt the practices of the community of faith of the *older* covenant. This will be discussed in chapter 6.

This description reminds us that we read the bible as part of the ongoing story of God. We read the Old Testament wearing our walking shoes of the Christian community to see how Jesus fulfils scripture. However, while the work of Christ on the cross was completed to achieve salvation for all people, the work of spreading the good news of this event is still incomplete. The message still needs to be delivered into all the world. The Christian community has the responsibility to continue this mission of the New Testament community in expanding the kingdom of God. As participants in this story we expect to follow in the footsteps of Jesus, empowered by the Spirit to witness to our Saviour. The shoes we wear are the shoes of readiness to spread the good news of Jesus Christ (Ephesians 6:15). This mandate can also be seen as a continuation of the older covenant testimony of the Abrahamic covenant: that through the seed of Abraham (Jesus Christ) all the nations of the earth will be blessed. The same God who was active in the lives of the ancient Israelite community is the same God who is active in the contemporary church. We read the Old Testament to help us in our mission and life together in Christian community. But the story did not end with the New Testament church. It continues, and will continue, as long as God is active in the world. In this ongoing story, we still await the final act when history will come to a close. As the story of God unfolds - from creation through Calvary and Pentecost to the present - each person has a part to play. You have a part to play in this magnificent story. This is why the third question is also crucial to consider as you read the Old Testament.

3. WHAT IS THE SIGNIFICANCE TO *ME*?

Our corporate identity as readers of the Old Testament is in positive continuity with ancient Israel and the New Testament people of God. Our lives and faith are situated in the context of the contemporary Christian church. But within this community, each of us plays a part. We are partners with God to transform both contemporary society and thus the future with the gospel. We discover our role in the activity of God as we take on the mantle of mission and evangelism from the New Testament writers and the Christian church. However in the midst of this, we each have our own individual struggles, concerns, faith and hope. By reflecting on the significance of the text for your personal life, you are appreciating the transformative power of the bible. Whenever we look to the Old Testament for faith, encouragement and guidance for our own lives,[5] we are asking: What is the significance of this for *me*? What is God saying to *me* through this passage? *Me*, who is part of the Christian community that is a continuation of the testimony of ancient Israel.

As we read the Old Testament, God speaks to each individual through the text. I'm not suggesting that there are dramatic trumpets blasting and golden sunlight beaming onto passages every time you read, but that there is a message, principle or example that is relevant for you in each reading. The bible speaks to each reader with insight into your own context and situation. As you read, the illumination of the biblical text by the Spirit is anticipated. By reading with an open heart and mind, the reader trusts the Holy Spirit to speak directly from the text of scripture into their own lives. While this will be further outlined in chapter 7, it is like you are wearing your own shoes. Having walked with the sandals of ancient Israel and the walking shoes of the New Testament community, your own shoes are representative of your unique situation and person. Therefore the significance of the biblical text to the individual reader – *me* – is a crucial element of this reading model. God may speak to you through the stories or vivid characters that help you to navigate life. Some characters, such as Daniel, Deborah and Joseph provide you with models of faith, courage and moral behaviour. Other characters are not so good, such as Solomon who begins as a wise and prosperous king but through his disastrous choices and marriages is transformed into a fool.[6] You can find guidance in the laws as they provide the foundation of ethical behaviour. The wisdom writings give you insight in how to negotiate relationships, work and family. The poetry of the Psalms and prophets can melt your heart as they stir you toward faith and obedience.

The significance of each question is crucial for readers to have a balanced perspective and balanced reading. To hear only *them*, or *us*, or *me* in isolation is to miss part of the testimony. We need all three testimonies of God at work to fully appreciate how the bible speaks to us. If we disregard or are ignorant of the voices of *them* and *us*, hearing only the voice of *me*, we can miss the fullness of what the bible is saying. Our readings become self-focused and we miss the point of God at work in the history of the world. All three pairs of shoes should be worn in your reading of the Old Testament to provide the boundaries of a responsible reading. How might this work?

Let's turn together to one of the most well-known passages in the Old Testament: Psalm 23. Once you have read the passage, think about the significance of this text to *them*, *us* and *me*. What did it mean for the ancient Israelite community? How might Jesus Christ and his followers have claimed this passage as part of their story? What is God saying to you personally through these words?

This Psalm was very important to *them* - the ancient Israelite community. It was a poem that described the nature and character of God through images common to their lifestyle and culture: shepherding (vv1-4) and feasting (vv5-6). The different types of writing, such as poetry, produced by the ancient community will be discussed in chapter 5. This passage is an example of poetry. It is a poem about God using concepts and images familiar to their ancient culture. For the agrarian society of ancient Israel, sheep were valued. Sheep were an essential part of the ancient Israelite economy because they can survive on a minimal amount of food and water, and can be moved to different grazing points. These sheep weren't fenced in and left to fend for themselves like some sheep farming today. They were completely dependant on the shepherd for protection, grazing, water, shelter and tending of injuries. They were completely helpless without their shepherd. That is why the shepherd was such a good model of care and compassion – they were guides, protectors and constant companions of the sheep as well as figures of authority and leadership to the animals under their care.[7] From this image, we can see characteristics about God that the Psalmist was trying to highlight for the ancient Israelite community. But that is not the only image used in this Psalm. A second image is presented in verse 5 of the poem as it describes a table spread with a banquet. But this is no ordinary feast; it is a feast fit for a king! Banquets and feasts in the Old Testament were representative of fellowship and celebration. The culmination of worship in the sacrificial system was the peace meal that emphasised the restoration of fellowship with God. This sense of peace and tranquillity is certainly evident in Psalm 23 as the guest is welcomed and honoured with generous gestures.

The combination of these images of a shepherd and feasting highlight the nature and character of God. They also highlight what the character and nature of God's representatives should be. The king of the ancient community was meant to represent God to the people. This poem is traditionally understood to have been written by King David. He was a shepherd before he ascended the throne. He ruled the people as a shepherd-king, reflecting God's ultimate reign. It is from this lineage of David that eventually another shepherd-king would come. This passage is significant to *us* in the Christian community because it points to Jesus Christ. Jesus described himself in John 10:11 as the "good shepherd". By saying this, he identified himself with God. While Jesus exhibits all the same characteristics of shepherds of the ancient community, he goes one step further. This shepherd will sacrifice his own life for the benefit of the sheep. So Jesus the good shepherd was crucified as the 'king of the Jews' (John 19:19). Once resurrected, Jesus appeared to the disciples. He encouraged those who would become leaders of this new community to be good shepherds of the flock and to feed the sheep (John 21:15-19). We remember the sacrifice of our shepherd-king as we share in the Lord's Table (Eucharist) – the celebration of the communion meal.

While this Psalm testifies to the character and nature of God, we can also read back into the poem from our New Testament perspective the sacrificial love of Jesus Christ. This message is highly significant to *me* as part of the Christian community. But its significance also goes a step further as I contemplate this passage for my own personal insight. What might God be saying to me through the text? What might God be saying to you through the Psalm? The answer depends on who you are! So while you reflect on what God might be saying to you through Psalm 23, I'll share its significance for me (Jacqui). This Psalm reminds me that wherever I journey in life I know that God will guide me. There have been different occasions in my life that required big decisions in my life-direction. The enormity of these decisions has felt overwhelming. I felt panicked in case I was making the wrong choice and was not hearing God correctly. As I look back I can see with security that God has guided me. Even when I was making a wrong decision, God clearly indicated that the path I had taken was the wrong way and gently guided me back as a good shepherd. Therefore this Psalm speaks to me of having a confidence in God to direct and guide me in decisions large and small. I can trust God, my good shepherd. I hope that as you reflect upon this Psalm it also inspires you with a similar confidence and hope. But this confidence comes through a knowledge of the culture and world of the ancient Issraelites. It is to this study that we now turn.

Group Discussion Questions:

1. Who is *them*?

2. What is the difference between *them* and *us*?

3. What would happen if you didn't bother to consider the significance of a passage for *them*?

4. Can you apply the 3 tools for reading to a specific passage? Without looking at the notes, try discussing how you might apply the tools to Psalm 1.

Recommended Reading:

ə Longman, T., *Making Sense of the Old Testament: Three Crucial Questions*, (Grand Rapids, Michigan: Baker, 1998).

This is a brilliant little book that asks three crucial questions about the Old Testament. It gives guidance in how to read as well as insight into some of the major concepts, such as covenant.

ə LaSor, W.S, Hubbard, D.A. & Bush, F.W., *Old Testament Survey: The Message, Form, and Background of the Old Testament*, 2nd Ed, (Grand Rapids, Michigan: Eerdmanns, 1996).

If you are after a thorough introductory survey of the Old Testament, then this is the book for you. It provides an overview of each of the 39 books, as well as some helpful information regarding issues in archaeology and historical matters.

ENDNOTES

1. Childs, B., *Biblical Theology of the Old and New Testaments*, (Minneapolis: Fortress, 1992), p.421.

2. Childs, B. *Biblical Theology of the Old and New Testaments*, p. 435.

3. Ricoeur, P., 'The Hermeneutics of Testimony' in Ricoeur, Paul, *Essays on Biblical Interpretations*, London: SPCK, 1981, p. 123.

4. Brueggemann, W., *Theology of the Old Testament: Testimony, Dispute, Advocacy*, (Minneapolis: Fortress Press, 1997), pp. 729-733.

5. Fee, G., 'History as Context for Interpretation' in Dyck, Elmer (ed) *The Act of Bible Reading*, (Downers Grove: Paternoster Press, 1996), p.11.

6. Longman, T., *Making Sense of the Old Testament: Three Crucial Questions*, (Grand Rapids, Michigan: Baker, 1998), p.14.

7. 'Sheep, Shepherd' in Ryken, L., Wilhoit, J.C. & Longman, T. (eds) *Dictionary of Biblical Imagery*, (Downers Grove: IVP, 1998), pp.782-784.

Chapter 4

THE SIGNIFICANCE FOR *THEM*:
SOCIAL WORLD OF THE ANCIENT ISRAELITES

The first question we have been asking as we read and explore a passage from the Old Testament, concerns the significance of the text to *them*. How was this testimony of God's actions important for the Old Testament community? The Old Testament presents the testimony of ancient Israel and their interaction with God. If we are willing to hear, we can learn from their experience. Through their testimony we can see God working for them and with them. Actually, the Old Testament is the collection of many voices and testimonies. Some of these voices are quite diverse. But what these testimonies show is that God is *with* the people and acts *for* the people – even when they didn't recognise it! The Old Testament was God's word to a specific people. God did not speak or act in a way they couldn't understand, but spoke their language. The Old Testament continually uses images and concepts that the people of that time understood. The writers used the conventions of their day to convey the truth of God's love and rule to them. They used images from daily life, such as shepherds, vineyards and pottery. They used images from their national life, such as sacrifices and covenant treaties.

Their worldview and culture affected what they thought, did and wrote. So we have to take their worldview and culture into consideration when reading the Old Testament. For example, to purchase property in ancient Israel during the time of Judges, the book of Ruth testifies of how Boaz went to the city gate to perform the transaction. As the male representative of the family, he had to enter negotiations on behalf of the widows Ruth and Naomi to save them from destitution. There was no social security system back then! As the proof of transaction for the property, Boaz exchanged sandals in the presence of the elders. In our culture and setting, real estate exchange is a very different process, so we can't just cut and paste ancient cultural norms onto our contemporary setting. While I can purchase a property in Australia, if I was a woman in ancient Israel I probably wouldn't be able to engage in property transactions (though I could inherit). In fact, the land wasn't seen as a commodity to be bought according to market forces but a gift from God stewarded by a family and subject to the rules of inheritance.[1] However what we glean from this testimony are important principles of honesty, responsibility and God's gracious kindness in providing for even the most overlooked people.

By hearing this testimony of the Old Testament people, we recognise that we are not ancient Israelites. We live in a different age and don't think the same way. We live in a very different culture and time. I do not have to swap shoes with my bank manager in order to buy a house (fortunately for both of us!). As we look at the cultural context of ancient Israel, this attention to historical matters makes us realise that we also are creatures of historical and social circumstances. As we read the Old Testament we become aware that we have our own historical context, which is different to the bible. Part of the dilemma for contemporary readers is that we are separated from this community in time and space. There is a gap between the events of the bible and today. So we can't ignore the cultural and historical differences between the world of the Old Testament and our own – we live in a completely different world. But by looking at the context, we can bridge that gap. When God speaks to you, it's in your own language and culture. If God spoke to you in Swahili or a language you didn't know, it would mean nothing to you. Actually it would make God seem removed and disinterested in you. When God speaks to us, it is in our language (for me, that's English). But not just our official language, God speaks to us in images and styles that are familiar to us and our world. So also God spoke to ancient Israel in the context of their historical, social and cultural situation.

To understand their life and culture better, there are three areas that we are going to look at: family life, political life and religious life. We will then briefly look at some of the religions and ideas of the surrounding nations to see how this religious life of ancient Israel was distinct from others. However before we look at these three areas of the ancient Israelite life and culture, consider for a moment your own family heritage. How would you describe your family? What kind of categories would you use to refer to them? When I think of my family, I think of my immediate family – my dad, mum, brother and sister. I also think of my mum's mother who died a few years ago that was very close to us. Although I have many aunts, uncles and cousins I am (unfortunately) not particularly close to them. To be honest, I probably think of my flatmates, friends and church friends as being closer than some of my blood relatives. While my family comes from the Blue Mountains near Sydney, they originate from Western Europe. My dad's heritage is mainly English (which must be why I love Earl Grey tea). My mum's heritage is French, Irish and English. Actually, my mum occasionally tries to convince us that her ancestors were French aristocrats who fled the Revolution to find refuge in England. Unfortunately we have no evidence for this beyond family legend. We don't really know much about our family history beyond a couple of hundred years at the most. This is very different for the ancient Israelites. As we reconstruct the family life and culture of *them* (ancient Israel), think about how your view of the world is either different or similar to the people described here.

1. FAMILY LIFE

Ancient cultures, generally, were group orientated. Women and men saw themselves not so much as individuals, but as members of a group. They worked and lived for the benefit of the group. While the life and blood of each individual was valued, the individual was generally not considered an autonomous being. They couldn't go off and do whatever they wanted (like the prodigal son) but would act and think for the benefit of the family. They were to bring honour to the group and avoid shame. Ancient Israelites were identified in relation to their community as part of a family, clan and tribe. This structure of their society was three-tiered. In Judges 6:15, God called Gideon to deliver Israel from the oppression of the Midianites. Gideon responds: "But Lord, how can I save Israel? My clan is the weakest in Manasseh, and I am the least in my family." He identifies himself as part of a household (or family), clan and tribe. This tribal system of ancient Israel was based on a common descent. They all identified themselves as being from the one descendant – Abraham, and from his heirs Isaac and Jacob. Jacob (sometimes called 'Israel') was the grandson of Abraham and the father of twelve sons who became known as the twelve tribes of Israel.

At each level, the community is led by a father or *pater*. This is how we get the term 'patriarchal'. It means that each group or level was under the authority of the father. The most foundational level is the family household. Much of their life was focused around this group. The household consisted of the father who was the head of the house, his wife and children. It also usually consisted of the married sons with their wives and children. Any unmarried aunts or the pater's widowed mother would also be included in this one household. This does not mean they all lived in the one house, but often in a several distinct houses within a unified compound. While buildings changed over time, the houses generally had two storeys. The bottom storey housed the livestock while the family lived on the second floor.[2] During the summer heat they might even sleep outside on the flat roof. The land that they cultivated was from their inheritance that would continue to be passed on to the children. The eldest son received a double portion and would become the family head at the death of the father.

The family lived together, worked together and learnt together. Each family member contributed to the household – even the children. The men were primarily responsible for the farming and animal husbandry. The children helped look after the livestock. The women were primarily responsible for the food production. This meant making the flour to bake the staple daily bread as each meal was produced from raw materials. However while the tasks were divided, there was a continual interaction of roles as needed. For example, at harvest time all the women and men worked in the fields (like the book of Ruth describes). This is why when a young girl married her family was given a dowry or bride-price. They were compensated for the loss of a worker. Even the children worked. The majority of the people were involved in some kind of agricultural work and would have all had a daily interaction with animals and livestock. The land was best suited to sheep and goats in the higher country, and these were often kept together (Matt.25:31-33). The shepherds kept the sheep more for wool than meat, so the relationship between them was often intimate and forged over years. It is no wonder that the image of God being like a shepherd was well used throughout scripture.

There was generally no formal schooling in ancient Israel so the education of children was the responsibility of the family and conducted in the home – by both father and mother. The book of Proverbs instructs sons (and daughters) to listen to both parents to receive wisdom, general knowledge and cultural values such as honesty (Proverbs 1:8). This included religious instruction. Hence education was not about learning to read or write as the majority of the population were illiterate. This helps explain the dominant use of poetry in the Old Testament. It was written to have an impact that was unforgettable and easily remembered. Sons would also be taught military skills from their fathers. A practice also required of men to be recognised as part of the covenant community was circumcision.

We do not have many pictures or illustrations of ancient Israelites, so it is difficult to know what they actually looked like. A lot of our data comes from the poetry and brief descriptions. However we do get the impression that the men were generally short and robust. They always wore a beard, but might shave the upper lip. Men of standing would often carry a staff. Their main garment was held by a sash. A cloak may have been worn for additional dignity and warmth. It could be taken in pledge for a debt, but had to be returned by nightfall as the owner slept in it (Deut 24:11-13). For example, Samuel received one new garment a year woven by his mother Hannah (1 Sam 2:19). The men usually also had a head covering (or turban). The women would wear a main garment or wrap that went under one arm and came forward from the back over the shoulder. Usually they would wear a head covering (though not a turban). They wore the same jewellery as men, though anklets, nose-rings and toe-rings were especially feminine adornments. According to scholars King and Stager, the life expectancy of a common person was less than 40. This was probably even lower for women who had to survive multiple childbirths without the help of modern medical practices.[3]

While the household was the basic unit in ancient Israelite society, the next level was the clan. Each village would have a council of elders who gathered at the town gate. The father of the household represented the family to the village clan. The clan leaders would discuss and decide on religious and legal matters. Legally the father or male head was responsible for the family. He was required to protect the family and represent them legally. The priority of the clan was the joint protection of the households. Most legal, military and economic functions were actioned through the clan. When a woman or dependant had no father to represent her, the closest blood relative within the clan (such as a brother or uncle) was required to act as her 'kinsman-redeemer'. For example, the law required the clan (rather than the tribe) to pursue blood revenge for murder when the father was unable (Numbers 35:19-27).

Marriages tended to be arranged by the families within the same clan. The women would then join her husband's family (contrary to the expectation in Genesis 2:24). This act of bringing the bride to the bridegroom's house was part of the ritual of the marriage ceremony (Genesis 24:67). While we are not sure of the age men and women married, scholars suggest that women generally married while in their teens, whereas men generally married in their mid to late twenties or even in their early thirties.[4] Divorce was permissible but uncommon. The chief goal of marriage, which tended to be more economically than romantically motivated, was to have and raise children.[5] Although it should be noted that some texts (such as the love poetry of 'Song of Songs') do celebrate the joy of sexual union. Children were highly valued as a blessing of God. Boys tended to be preferred as they could continue the family and the father's name.[6] In contrast, barrenness or infertility was considered a curse.

While the clans varied in size, there was probably an average of fifty clans that can be established for each tribe. The clan leaders would represent their group in the tribal gatherings. Each tribe had its own name. This name was derived from its ancestor who was one of Jacob's sons. The tribes tended to be regional, although they were not uniform in their population or geographic size. In other words, each household and clan lived in a particular geographic area allocated to their tribe (Joshua 13-22). The allocation came from the time of the Conquest as the book of Joshua testifies to the division of the land into twelve areas. Each tribe was given a land allocation (except the Levites which will be discussed below). It was from the tribe that resources for their corporate, or national, existence were drawn. It was from the tribe that volunteer, and later conscript, armies were drawn. These warriors were motivated by the protection of their clans and families. Being part of a tribe gave the members a sense of identity and tribal honour. The contribution to tribal protection and expansion was important since warfare was a common reality in the history of ancient Israel. Because ancient Israel was located on the main trade route between Egypt and Mesopotamia they were vulnerable to attack from their neighbours. However, as King and Stager note, "when the North (Israel) and the South (Judah) were not fighting a common enemy, they were fighting each other."[7]

The tribe also provided leadership. It was the tribal leaders who would settle large and more difficult disputes. However this was later displaced by the royal administration. Yet, despite this, tribal identity was still strong. Family heritage and tribal allegiances were very important to them. That is why there are genealogies scattered throughout the Old Testament. Their heritage from Abraham and continuation of his promise and blessings was valued. This promise and blessing also included the land in which they dwelt. The physical characteristics of the region inhabited by the tribes were quite diverse – from broad plains to mountainous regions. The area of the southern kingdom (Judah) was characterised by its narrow valleys filled with great rocks. The area of the northern kingdom, particularly Samaria, was marked by broad plains. Hence the Assyrians were able to conquer the northern kingdom with relative ease, while Judah was more difficult to take. The physical features also help explain the frequent Israelite disunity. The land was more suitable for tribal possessions or city-states than a strongly united nation. Because it never controlled the coastal plain and was landlocked, ancient Israel did not develop as a maritime people.

2. POLITICAL LIFE

Even when systems of government changed (such as from theocracy in Judges to monarchy) and social change occurred, such as urbanization and development of class divisions, the social structure remained basically intact. For example, when the Jews returned to Jerusalem from their exile in Babylon, according to the testimony of Ezra 2 they still had documents giving details of their lineages and tribal identity. However as we continue to look at the cultural context of ancient Israel, it is important at this point to recognise that while we can generalise about this group of people called "ancient Israel", it was not a static society. In other words, it didn't stay the same but was a constantly changing culture and society. This is particularly true of their political life and organisation. This was usually due to the development of technology within the nation and the influence of the culture and technology from the surrounding nations. For example, when we read the accounts of Abraham, the society it describes is nomadic. That is, they were a wandering tribe, roaming from pasture to pasture. They lived in tents and mainly looked after livestock such as sheep. After the exodus from Egypt, this family had grown into a nation. Their testimony tells us that during the time of the conquest (Joshua) they became a pastoral society. They were fixed to the land and began farming as well as maintaining livestock. Thus the life of the people began to be more and more focused on the cities.

With the rise of Saul, we can see a transition to a monarchy (being ruled by a king) which was established by David and completed under Solomon. Having a king meant that there was a capital city with a palace and all the trappings of royal life. Despite this the majority of the people were still involved in some kind of agricultural work. The monarchy transformed ancient Israel into a social pyramid, where the upper class ruled the lower class masses. It is often described as the urban elite on the top (these were the administrators, rich landowners, and the royal establishment) while the rural masses and peasants were on the bottom. This class division was further emphasised throughout the monarchic period. The rich got richer and more exclusive, and the poor got poorer. This led to the rise of a unique ministry of the prophets. Many of the prophets spoke out against the rich and their injustice towards the poor. This was especially because the rich sometimes violated the covenant laws to achieve their wealth. After the exile they still continued to be an agricultural or pastoral society whose administration was centred on the cities. So while we can generalise about how they lived, it was not always the same throughout this changing period we call 'Old Testament times'. This is also true of their worship.

3. Religious Life

Worship was central to the experience of ancient Israel in relating to God. Their worship was expressed in concrete acts performed by the community. Their worship contained rituals and structure. However these rituals were an outward form designed to reflect the inner cleansing of the heart. The goal was to honour and reflect the nature or character of the God they served – God's holiness. The way they expressed this was through the sacrificial or Levitical system. This system had sacred space, sacred people to administer the worship, and sacred sacrifices.

The first books of the Old Testament describe the use of sacred altars where worship was conducted by the head of the family (Gen.12:8; 13:8). At the time of the exodus, however, the people of God were no longer an extended family, but a mighty nation. Because of this Moses was commanded to build a tabernacle so that God might be approached in worship. The tabernacle became their portable worship centre, and symbolised that God had come to live among his covenant people. Here ancient Israel could worship and fellowship with God. Later, when they lived permanently in the land, the tabernacle was replaced with the Temple, a permanent structure in Jerusalem.

It should come as no surprise to learn that the sacred spaces of ancient Israel had similar features to the temples of the other nations in the ancient Near Eastern world. Many had courtyards where worshippers could congregate and inner holy places where only priests could go. But unlike other Temples, the ancient Israelite Tabernacle (and Temple) did not have images – they contained no images because the living God manifested his presence in the innermost room where his glory dwelled (Exodus 40:34-35). The New Testament tells us that in Jesus Christ, the Word became flesh and tabernacled among us (Jn.1:14). The body of Jesus was likened by John to this tent that contained the glory of the Lord. When Jesus cleansed the Temple (John 2:13-33) he said, "Destroy this Temple, and I will raise it up in three days." After his resurrection the disciples figured out he was talking about his body. So when the religious and political authorities destroyed that temple (the physical body of Jesus), they also destroyed the actual temple in Jerusalem as the curtain in the Holy Place was torn in two. There ended the Levitical system of worship. But through the Spirit, each of us believers have also become part of the temple of God (1 Cor.3:16-17; 6:19). Consequently for the Christian church, there is no central holy place where believers must attend and enter with ritual. This doesn't mean we can't set apart places or buildings for spiritual use, but they are only commemorative.

The worship system of ancient Israel contained not only sacred space but sacred people. These people were called 'priests'. They were given specific roles and responsibilities in the tabernacle to administer the worship and acted as mediators between God and the people. They were distinguished by specific clothing that they wore. These clothes signified their status as representatives of God to the people, and representing the people to God. Some of their tasks included performing and overseeing the ritual sacrifices and maintaining the tabernacle. The priests were also responsible for instructing the people regarding the content and application of the law. These sacred people were taken from one of the twelve tribes of ancient Israel: the Levites. Because they were dedicated to God's service they did not receive a land inheritance, but were provided for by the offerings and gifts of the people. From these priests there was appointed a High Priest who would perform specific rituals such as on the Day of Atonement. Because it was necessary to have a High Priest to go into the presence of God and to atone for sin and make intercession for the community, Jesus has become our High Priest and makes intercession for us (Hebrews 4:14-5:10).

The concept of sacred people and sacrificial ritual was also widespread in the ancient Near Eastern world. So when God instituted the sacrifices, it was a form the people were familiar with.

In fact, the biblical texts don't even explain it comprehensively – it assumes the people knew the process and structure. The sacrifices were primarily conducted in the Temple – the place of God's presence. They provided ancient Israel a means of approaching the Lord through the sacrifice of an animal that was offered on their behalf. The specifics of these sacrifices, such as the sin offering, guilt offerings and peace offerings are outlined in the book of Leviticus. Although the sacrificial system of ancient Israelite worship was quite complex, there are some central characteristics highlighted by Allen Ross in his commentary on Leviticus. He highlights that the sacrifices were an expression of gratitude and devotion to God.[8] It acknowledged that God was sovereign and everything belonged to God anyway. The sacrifices expressed communion and relationship with God.

Also essential to the religious life of ancient Israel were the annual feasts. These festivals emphasised the role of the family in transmitting their religion through stories and songs. For example, the Passover meal was part of the religious instruction where the children would ask their parents the meaning of the special meal. As the story of the exodus was retold, the people would remember and celebrate their deliverance. As the traditional calendar of feasts is connected to their agricultural life it also emphasised the holistic view of their faith. Covenant faith and obedience was the guarantee for the seasonal rains and blessing of abundance (Deuteronomy 28). The land produced with God's blessing through suitable seasons their staples such as grain, wine and oil (Deut.7:13; Ps.104:15; Hos.2:8; Joel 2:19). Wheat and barley were the main grain crops. There was, and is, a fairly predictable pattern of rain. From May to September/October there was little rain. The land depended upon dew and morning mist. The early rains from September/October could often be very heavy and softened the ground ready for ploughing. The latter rains in March/April came just when needed during the time of reaping (Deut.11:13-14; Ps.65:9-13; Jer.5:24).[9]

However ancient Israel did not live in a vacuum, but interacted with the wider culture and surrounding nations. They were located in a narrow strip of land next to the Mediterranean, and surrounded by neighbours of alternative religious traditions. We tend to think of ancient Israel as being the most significant nation in the ancient world, but this was far from the perception of the time. Ancient Israel at this time was a latecomer to international politics. That made them a minor player in the arena of international politics and culture dominated by Egypt, Assyria and Babylon. Throughout its history, ancient Israel was in contact with neighbouring peoples and was familiar with their chief literary works, and also the mindset or worldview of their neighbours. Ancient Israel was surrounded by nations that were polytheistic – they worshipped many gods. This was a continual temptation for them. Throughout the Old Testament, ancient Israel was continually challenged to reject the religion of the nations around them and worship the one true God. As Deuteronomy 6:14 says: "you must not worship any of the gods of neighbouring nations, for the Lord your God, who lives among you, is a jealous God" (TNIV). Sometimes they succeeded and turned from the worship of idols and 'foreign' gods, and sometimes they did not succeed. This challenge is dominant throughout every period in the history of ancient Israel as recorded in the Old Testament. Ancient Israel was always susceptible to, and regularly embraced, the idolatry of their neighbouring nations.

One of the most tempting gods for ancient Israel was the Canaanite god, Ba'al. Ba'al (which just means 'master' or 'lord') was considered the god of storm and rain. He was also sometimes called 'the rider on the clouds', like God in Ps 68:5.[10] The worship of Ba'al was a constant temptation for ancient Israel as they were dependant on the right rains in the right season for successful crops. Could their God of the exodus provide them with this rain or should they trust in the Ba'al of the local people? Why not both (just in case)? In contrast, the Egyptians worshipped the sun-god Amon-Re. Each day Amon-Re would rise from the Sea of Reeds having defeated the

chaos in the water, bringing light and life to the land of Egypt. The
land was stewarded to Amon-Re's son, the Pharaoh, who was made
in his image.

In contrast, the Mesopotamian gods were much like their
geographic environment: harsh and unpredictable. Their creation
story (called the *Enuma Elish*) shows the Babylonian mindset of
pessimism and fear of their environment. The poem *Enuma Elish* tells
of the birth of the gods through Apsu, the male principal god and
Tiamat, the female principal god. Tiamat wants to destroy the young
gods, who are disturbing her. The young gods hear of it, so delegate
power to Marduk (the god of Babylon) to defend them. Marduk
kills Tiamat and the gods allied with her, forming the world from her
body. Marduk then sets some other gods the task of building him a
home in Babylon. However, they protest at the thought of manual
labour. So Marduk kills another god, Kingu, and uses his blood to
create humankind.[11] Humans are thus created to do the work that
the gods don't want to do. Compare this in your mind with Genesis
1 in which the Lord creates humanity with dignity and purpose. We
see also that in this Babylonian story, the gods are not noble or good,
but petty and selfish.[12]

When we compare the rituals and religious system of ancient
Israel with the surrounding nations of the ancient Near Eastern world,
we see that many of the forms that were given to ancient Israel would
have been familiar to them. All aspects of their worship rituals have
parallels in the cultures of the ancient world: sacred ground, temples,
sacrifices, priests. Does this interaction with other nations and the
use of some of their forms of worship mean the bible is not unique?
Why did God institute the Levitical system as the form of worship?
Is God just interested in killing animals? Although we observe that
the form was similar, their focus and content was very different. The
focus of ancient Israel was on the one true and living God. So while
they used the same method of the peoples around them, the purpose
was different. These methods were not just adopted but adapted for

the special purpose of worshipping the creator of the universe. It can be likened to the contemporary music used in many churches today. Although generally the style of music in some contemporary worship originates from non-Christian sources, it is adapted for the purposes of worship. This can also be seen in the writings of ancient Israel that sometimes had similarities in style to their neighbours. This will be discussed in the next chapter.

GROUP DISCUSSION QUESTIONS:

1. What is the tribal structure? In your group, make a chart that shows what the tribal structure looked like.

2. What questions would you ask of an ancient Israelite?

3. How is the God of Israel different to the gods of the other nations?

4. Read Judges 6:1-16. Apply the 'tools of the trade' to this passage:

    i.   What is the significance to *them*?
    ii.   What is the significance to *us*?
    iii. What is the significance to *me*?

RECOMMENDED READING

❧ Gower, Ralph, *Student Handbook to Manners and Customs of Bible Times*, (Carlisle: Candle Books, 2000)

This is a great little book that is not only inexpensive but very helpful. It has a good balance of information and illustrations. It is recommended for readers who want an introduction to some of the general aspects of culture represented in the bible.

❧ Craigie, P.C., *The Old Testament: Its background, Growth, & Content,* (Nashville: Abingdon, 1992)

This is a much heavier book than the example above. It discusses the culture of the Old Testament thematically and is a good source of information.

❧ King, Philip J. & Stager, Lawrence E., *Life in Biblical Israel,* (Louisville: Westminster/John Knox Press, 2001)

This is an excellent book that is very detailed. It is an academic book, so if you are looking for light reading, the first of these recommendations is better for you. However, if you really want solid research and archaeological examination, then this book is for you.

ENDNOTES:

1. King, P.J. & Stager, L.E., *Life in Biblical Israel,* (Louisville: Westminster/John Knox Press, 2001), p.193.

2. King, P.J. & Stager, L.E., *Life in Biblical Israel,* p. 28.

3. King, P.J. & Stager, L.E., *Life in Biblical Israel,* p.37.

4. King, P.J. & Stager, L.E., *Life in Biblical Israel,* p.38.

5. King, P.J. & Stager, L.E., *Life in Biblical Israel,* p. 54.

6. King, P.J. & Stager, L.E., *Life in Biblical Israel,* p.42.

7. King, P.J. & Stager, L.E., *Life in Biblical Israel,* p.223.

8. Ross, Allen P., *Holiness to the Lord: A Guide to the Exposition of the Book of Leviticus,* (Grand Rapids, Michigan: Baker Academic, 2002), p. 73.

9. King, P.J. & Stager, L.E., *Life in Biblical Israel,* p.88.

10. Charpentier, E., *How to Read the Bible: The Old and New Testaments,* (New York: Gramercy Books, 1981), p.19.

11. Enns, P., *Inspiration and Incarnation: Evangelicals and the Problem of the Old Testament,* (Grand Rapids, Michigan: Baker Academic, 2005), p.26.

12. Charpentier, E., *How to Read the Bible: The Old and New Testaments,* p.18.

Chapter 5

THE SIGNIFICANCE FOR *THEM*:
A WRITING COMMUNITY

We have noted in our description of the Old Testament so far that it is a collection of testimonies. These testimonies were collected over a long period of time and preserved by the ancient Israelite, Jewish and Christian communities. They were arranged in an order that reflects the theology of each of the communities. We have also noted that not all of these testimonies within the Old Testament are the same. These various testimonies collected are very different in their style and type of writing. So the bible is both a single book, but also a library of books with all kinds of writings and all sorts of writing styles. These writing styles were deliberately chosen and used by the ancient Israelite community to testify to God's actions among them. For this reason it is crucial that we are not only mindful of the *culture* of the community that produced these writings, but also the *types* of writings they produced.

Because the testimonies are all different, it is important to recognise their unique style of writing. This identification of each style of writing of a biblical text is called its 'genre' (pronounced "john–ra"). It sounds a very technical term, but basically refers to a particular style or way of writing. It comes from the French to mean 'general'.[1] There are general similarities that types of writing have. Examples of different genres in our world include: poetry, prose (or story), recipes, mystery novels, instruction manuals, diary entries, essays, sermons, dictionary entries. Often we identify different genres without even realising. It is something that you intuitively recognise all the time. So although 'genre' may be a strange word to you, it is something that you do all the time. Consider the following pieces of writing. What genre would you identify them as?

1. Once upon a time lived a rich king....
2. Dear diary, today I read the best book ever about how to read the Old Testament.....
3. Two men armed with high calibre weapons ...
4. Shall I compare thee to a summer's day? Thou art more lovely and more temperate....
5. Dear Jacqui, thank you for your invitation to your birthday party ...
6. Step 1: Set the oven to 180 degrees. Step 2: take a cup of sifted flour....

These are six very different types of writing. They all use a different form or style to convey their message. Their 'genre' is different. The first example is in the general style of a fairy story or fable. How did you identify it as a fairy story? The use of the words "once upon a time" are like a trigger to tell you that this is not a historical account but a fanciful story that is not based on real events. It presents a world outside of time. Yet while it may not be 'historical fact', it will usually contain some truth in the moral of the story. It is an identifiable, unique type of writing. The second example is also quite unique. It is a diary entry. It provides a subjective account of personal experience presented as a reflection on the day's events. It is very different to the third example of a newspaper report.

The genre of a newspaper article can be identified by its presentation of a report. Its purpose is to inform the reader in a quick and concise way of events and issues relevant to them. As a report, it includes quotes and perspectives from eye witnesses and experts. It is usually formatted in easy to read columns with photographs that confirm the information in the report. The report genre is very unromantic and objective in comparison to the fourth type of writing:

a poem. Poetry is identified by its use of images and literary devices such as metaphors. Poetry is very compact. It says a lot with very few words. Yet perhaps what is most unique about poetry is that it stirs the emotions of the reader as they think on the words and images described. It is not literal. The woman is not literally a sunny day, but there is something warm and luminous about her that reminds the writer of a summer's day. This particular sonnet of Shakespeare stirs our hearts and imaginations. Again, it is very different to the fifth example of a formal letter. It has a unique form in that it is addressed to a particular person. This example conveys a specific and polite message of acceptance to an invitation. In comparison, politeness is very far from the intentions of the last example of genre. A recipe is deliberately short and demanding. It commands the reader to obey the instructions of each step precisely.

Identifying the genre, or type of writing, is very important. Every culture and community has to create different ways of communicating for different occasions and purposes. This was also true of ancient Israel. They have created all different ways of expressing their testimony of God's actions in and through their community. They expressed this through stories, laws, poetry, parables, epics, prophetic oracles, teachings and wisdom writings.[2] Each mode of expression conveys a message and truth in a different way. We need to ask what kind of truth or message each particular genre presents. A fairytale may not be 'true' in the historical or literal sense, but its moral and message may be true.[3]

The testimonies of the Old Testament were deliberately written by the ancient community using particular forms of writing. While you may not have considered this concept of genre before, the choice of the form of writing very much reflects the message and the meaning. This means we must pay close attention to what genre or form of writing is being used to know how we should interpret the passage. This is crucial because you don't read a recipe the same way you would read a fairy story. Likewise, when you read a poem, you don't read it as a historical account. As Tremper Longman notes, the genre indicates the reading strategy.[4] The kind of genre a piece of literature is, determines how it should be read and understood. For example, if I switched the genres of some of the above examples, it affects what kind of message I am presenting and how you understand its meaning.

7. Step 1: note the current summer weather. Step 2: compliment lover using the weather pattern noted above.

How does the change in genre effect the change in message? What was a beautiful, passionate and charming comparison in the Shakespeare sonnet becomes cold, sterile and calculating when presented like a recipe. It becomes a recipe for romantic disaster!

Similarly when I try to present the instructions for a recipe as a romantic poem the message becomes confused:

8. Fire burning deep and bright; Blackened tomb flamed with light.

Poetry aims to stir your heart and intellect through its imagery. It requires you to use your imagination. While I might intend from these lines to convey the instruction of setting the oven to a very hot temperature, the exactness of the message is lost in the description. This is because poetry uses imagery rather than necessarily being literal. It becomes a description and suggestion at most, rather than the directive of a recipe. If any of you have seen me in the kitchen, I already struggle to create culinary delights from exact instructions without being further confused by vagueness.

These examples highlight how the genre indicates the reading strategy. When we read the bible it is important that we identify the genre. For example, when we open up the book of Ezra and read chapter 6:1-2:

King Darius then issued an order, and they searched in the archives stored in the treasury at Babylon. A scroll was found

in the citadel of Ecbatana in the province of Media, and this
was written on it: Memorandum: In the first year of King
Cyrus the king issued a decree concerning the Temple of God
in Jerusalem.... (TNIV).

It presents a historical account - that is the genre. Therefore we must
read the passage in this way. Why is it significant to *them*? It presents
a historical account or testimony of the way God moved the heart
of a Persian king after the exile of the Judeans to Babylon. God
moved his heart to allow the Jewish people to return to Jerusalem,
rebuild the Temple and re-establish worship in their own land. It
is significant to *us* because from this group of returned exiles, the
saviour of the world, Jesus Christ would come. It is significant to *me*
personally because it reminds me that God can move even the heart
of a pagan king to see his purposes fulfilled.

However, just as the last chapter noted that the cultural
world of ancient Israel was very different to our own, so also can
be their literary categories. When we look at the genre of 'history'
in ancient books, we must be careful not to impose our modern
understanding of history onto the text. Ancient histories didn't try
to give an objective account of events. Instead, the events of the Old
Testament are reported to us in the form of a testimony. They are a
theological interpretation of events. This does not mean that they are
not true, or historically unreliable. What they present is a testimony
or report of events from a theological perspective. For example,
a few years ago during our orientation week at Southern Cross
College, I was talking to a student and asked them how they came
to study with us. They said: "God brought me here". As I queried
them further, I discovered that they had been made redundant from
their job so they were looking for a new purpose. At the same time,
someone unexpectedly offered to buy their house in another city
where they had been living. Throughout this time, they felt that
God had been directing them to get some theological training and
ministry preparation. In fact, they felt that God had been speaking

to them about this idea for over a year, but they always used their job and home as an excuse. These circumstances confirmed to them that now was the time and opportunity to follow God's leading to go to College and be prepared for the next season in their life.

Now if I was writing the account of this student in the form of a contemporary 'modern history', I would interpret the events from a materialist perspective in chronological order. I would narrate how they felt a call to ministry, lost their job, sold their house, moved to Sydney and went to theological college. Is that what happened? Yes. Well, actually, yes and no. From a theological perspective, this student had committed their future to God who (in the unseen realm) was directing events to enable them to fulfil the calling on their life for ministry. That is the theological interpretation of events, or testimony. So when this student answered my question of why they were at College, their answer: "God brought me here" is a theological interpretation of events or their testimony. This is very much like the historical accounts in the Old Testament. They present a theological view. The histories of ancient Israel are the report or testimony of God's unseen activity in their seen world.

Another type of writing, or genre, used frequently in the Old Testament is poetry. When we open up the book of Psalms (for example) and read in the first chapter:

Blessed are those who do not walk in the counsel of the wicked

Or stand in the way of sinners

Or sit in the seat of mockers. (TNIV)

We are not reading a historical account, but poetry. So if genre indicates the reading strategy, we read it the way it is mean to be read. Poetry uses imagery and poetic devices. It is not meant to be exact or literal, but to stir our hearts, will and emotions as well as our minds.[5] This Psalm begins by using a negative metaphor to describe the type of person who is considered 'righteous'. In other words, the kind of person that is in right relationship with God. However this

Psalm describes the righteous person through contrasts. It begins by highlighting what the blessed or righteous person is *not*. They are not someone who associates with wickedness. In fact, the first three lines present the same idea of associating with wickedness but increasingly intensified. This literary device of having parallel ideas in a poem is called 'parallelism'. The second line reinforces or even intensifies the first line. The concept of the righteous person in Psalm 1 is not just an abstract concept, but a concrete reality. This reality is demonstrated by the image of a person who increasingly entrenches themselves in a wrong lifestyle as they move from walking to standing to sitting with the ungodly. The use of movement in the imagery is memorable as it intensifies their moral decline. It was important for Hebrew poetry to have impacting imagery since most of the population were illiterate and had to memorise these truths. Of course, while it is an image, is not too hard to visualise someone engaging with the wicked and wicked practices as they journey through life. This is the main idea of Psalm 1 – it shows us which path we should walk in order to live a life blessed by God. This has implications not just here on earth, but also into eternity.

As the Psalm continues, it identifies a righteous person as one who looks to the Lord for their guidance, it says:

> But their delight is in the law of the Lord,
>
> and on his law they meditate day and night.
>
> They are like trees planted by streams of water,
>
> which yield their fruit in season
>
> and whose leaves do not wither.
>
> Whatever they do prospers. (TNIV)

The person blessed by God meditates and delights in the law. This is not what we normally associate with the Old Testament law. We tend to think of the law as the complete opposite to grace. While the word 'torah' can mean law, it can also more generally mean 'guidance'. This helps us to understand the purpose and intent of the law in the Old Testament. It was meant to guide the people in right relationship with God and others. So this righteous person finds delight and security in the guidance of God to which they look consistently (as represented by 'day and night'). To understand the blessed state of this person, the Psalmist compares them to a tree. This is a very significant picture or image to use. They are not saying that the righteous person is literally a tree, but they are making a comparison. This is called a simile. A simile uses words to make a comparison explicit. It will describe something being 'like' or 'as'. For example, someone might describe you "as sweet as pie". Whereas a metaphor makes the comparison implicit. It doesn't use 'as' or 'like' but just states the subject as being the image (such as "the Lord is my shepherd").

This tree is highly significant as a comparison to the righteous person. This tree is a picture of security, health, vitality and generosity. This is what the righteous person is like. The tree is not just any random tree but is strategically placed. It is described as being planted by the rivers of water. The tree has constant nourishment and a ready source of life in times of drought. This tree is described as fruitful. It reproduces itself through fruit and seed as it provides for others beyond its own needs. Yet this fruit is produced in the reliability and fullness of the right season. The health of the tree is further emphasised by the reference to its leaves that have not withered but remained strong and green. This is what a righteous person is like. Yet, the righteous person is not literally a tree. However, the picture of what this tree is like gives us insight into what a follower of God is like.

The Psalm continues to compare the blessed with the ungodly. The ungodly is next described as being like chaff. Chaff is the exterior husk that contained the wheat kernel. The farmer winnows the wheat to remove the chaff from the husk so that it can be destroyed. The chaff has no value and no use. That is where the pathway of the ungodly leads. The poem draws the reader into the world of the images to persuade them to follow the wise path of obedience of God's guidance. In that path they find blessing, security and life.

By drawing on imagery from everyday life, such as nature (trees), pathways and farming life (chaff), the poet describes the unknown through the known. The comparison works because I may not know anything about a righteous person, but I know something about trees. By reflecting on what a tree is like I can understand something of this blessed and righteous person. But these comparisons in Psalm 1 are interesting. Why compare the blessed person to a tree? Why a tree and not a rock, or a lion, or an aeroplane? A rock has security, but not the life and vitality of a tree. A lion has the vitality but is unpredictable and not perceived to be generous. Aeroplanes were not invented then so would have been meaningless to the people of ancient Israel as a comparison. But a tree exemplifies the qualities of vitality, security and blessing that can be found in a righteous person.

The Old Testament poets and prophets often used language relevant to the people. They drew on images common and known to the people. While we have our own images, the culture of the ancient Near Eastern world had its own contemporary images that were ingrained in their culture.[6] Images depicting the gods as warriors were fairly well-known. For example, these images were utilised in the bible and describe God in battle array and leading the army of hosts into victory for the people (such as Joshua 5:13-15). They picture God marching down in anger – accompanied by storms, dark clouds, thunder, lightning and heavy rain (Judges 4-5). His appearance affects the cosmos as the earth quakes and the Lord's enemies melt in fear or run away. Other images describe God as a mother eagle, father and king.

The poetry of Psalm 1 is significant to *them* because it speaks their language and culture. Not just in the ancient Hebrew, from which we have translated this poem, but in imagery easily accessible to them. The poem speaks of God's law and guidance as a positive life-giving observance. It compels and persuades the ancient community towards faith and obedience. They have a choice of two paths; this wisdom poem encourages them to take the path of blessing and obedience. As they follow God's law and plan, then they will be blessed as the Torah promises in Deuteronomy 28. Yet this life of obedience for the ancient Israelites wasn't dreary or dull, but fruitful and satisfying. This same choice is offered by Christ. This makes the passage significant for *us*. We can take the path of life or reject this offer to follow the path of the ungodly. The New Testament tells us that Christ offers the pathway to faith and blessing through himself. Jesus identified himself as the way, the truth and the life (John 14:6). We find the path of blessing not through our own righteousness or good works, but through faith in Jesus Christ. Yet, while this image can represent the bigger picture of our ultimate destiny in God, it can also refer to the specific journey of each believer as they attempt to live in faithfulness to the guidance of God. In this way, it is also significant for *me* (and you). The decisions we make can lead us either down the path of the ungodly, or along the way of the righteous. As we choose to listen and follow the guidance from God, we too can experience the blessing of the righteous person as represented by the tree. We can have a security and vitality in God that overflows into fruitfulness and generosity.

Yet poetry and historical narrative are not the only types of genre used in the Old Testament. There are a multitude of different forms and writings utilised by the ancient community to testify to God's actions among them. Another important form of literature was the 'prophetic oracle'. Although the prophets often used the poetic form, it was utilised for the purpose of calling the people back to God. They challenged the leaders and the community when they disobeyed God, and encouraged them with words of hope and promise when they were faithful. However when the people were disobedient, their words were expressed as judgement. The impending judgement was a result of the people's disobedience of the covenant and rejection of God's ways. Yet, these prophetic utterances were not just any words. The prophets spoke on behalf of God to the community. Their aim was to direct the people onto the pathway outlined by God, particularly through the guidance of the law. As God's spokespeople, their words had a powerful effect in directing the course of ancient Israel's history.[7] God used them to speak to the people using images and language relevant to them. Their words were mainly recorded as poetry because their message was intended to be vivid, memorable and easily remembered for an oral society.

This is seen in Isaiah 40:1-5, which presents a vibrant and memorable message of hope. This section of Isaiah is understood to have been addressed to the Judeans (southern kingdom) exiled to Babylon and separated from their homeland. They had rejected God time and time again, bringing the judgement of their rejection upon themselves. All along, throughout the previous chapters of Isaiah the threatened punishment for disobedience was exile and destruction by the surrounding nations. This is consistent throughout the Old Testament, beginning with Deuteronomy: if the people sinned against God (if they violated the covenant) then they would heap the curses of the covenant upon themselves. The most feared of these threats was the removal from the land. This is exactly what happened in the exile. But despite this, God did not forget them. This section of Isaiah anticipates the restoration of the people. It promises the comfort that they so desperately needed in their banishment. It is introduced by the repetition of the words in 40:1- "comfort, comfort". The prophet implores the dejected and defeated people through the poetry to be encouraged or 'take heart'. The Lord speaks words of comfort to 'my people' through the prophet. They are not rejected. Despite all that has happened, they are still God's people.

This suggests that this prophetic text is a message of comfort for those in exile. The time of exile is ended. They have paid the price, and it's now time to return home. The call for 'comfort' is for the current generation. It is not just a future hope, but a present reality. This section in Isaiah then describes a voice calling in the wilderness. Like Psalm 1, it uses the image of a pathway. This is a prophetic voice that pictures metaphorically a wilderness with a highway through it. On this highway, God will flatten every obstacle and raise any depression in their journey to bring back the exiles. God will return his people to himself through this pathway he is creating straight through the wilderness. On this highway God will march, and with him will walk the remnant, the home-comers. In the earlier Ezra passage we saw reference to how God would create this 'highway': in that the pagan king whose heart was moved by God would release and help the Judean people. This message was significant to *them*, the people of ancient Israel, because it meant that God had not abandoned them to exile and judgement forever. Although they may have felt rejected and defeated, God was bringing them back and restoring them as a people. It was a new work that God was doing. It says to *them*: God is coming to act powerfully on behalf of Judah to bring them home and leave Babylon. In this new work, God is asserted as the powerful agent who is greater than Babylon and Persia (and their gods).

But this is not the only time that we will hear this voice in the bible. These same words were used later by the gospel writers to describe the role and message of John the Baptist (Matthew 3). Like the prophet in Isaiah 40, John the Baptist also proclaimed a message of a new work of God. God was creating a new pathway to restore relationship with himself through Jesus Christ. So Matthew used the words of Isaiah to speak of the new work God was doing. While the words of Isaiah were still important and relevant to the original hearers of ancient Israel (this will be further discussed in chapter 11), they were used in a new and fresh way in the New Testament. For Matthew, it would not be a literal highway in the desert but a new pathway created which no longer required the sacrifices of the old system. Instead this pathway was created through the giving of the Son to restore right relationship on our behalf. We no longer need to be in exile from God, but God has made a way to bring us back to him through faith in Jesus Christ. That is also the significance of the text to *us.* Yet the power of poetry means that this passage speaks to us not only with this essential message to ancient Israel (*them*) and to the New Testament community (*us*) but continues to speak in dynamic ways to each reader (*me*). These exact same words were used by Martin Luther King Jnr in his 'I have a Dream' speech to present an alternative reality to the racial and social injustice experienced in North America in the 1960s. He used these very words of Isaiah to describe his hope of social equality within the community and announce a new vision of reality.[8] This passage may also speak to you personally of a new work of transformation and change that God is doing or going to do within your life, Church or community.

There were many other types of writings produced by the ancient Israelite community that will be discussed in Part II of this book, but it is important at this point to acknowledge some of the many varied genres. There are family stories or narratives (such as Abraham's call in Genesis 12) that speak of the experience of the ancestors of the ancient Israelite community. Wisdom literature has many forms. Some wisdom writings, such as Proverbs 10-30 present pithy, practical sayings. They are easy to remember and generally deal with everyday life and relationships. They are short, catchy little sayings that offer good advice. Other wisdom writings, however, such as Job, are written more like a dialogue as they engage the bigger questions of life's meaning and the nature of suffering. The laws (such as Exodus 20) give specific direction and definite boundaries to the community in their interaction socially, legally and politically. They are generally written in the imperative; a command to be obeyed rather than a suggestion. Each of these types of writing (whether poetry, narrative or law) present the testimony, experience and knowledge of the community in a specific way. They are not all the same and not meant to be read the same way, but each are valued for their input.

It is true that sometimes the genre of a passage in the Old Testament is not always clearly identifiable. Sometimes passages are a combination of two or more types of writings, such as the prophetic oracles. A text may reflect multiple genres. However, the task of identifying the genres acknowledges that there were specific types of writing important to the ancient Israelite community and produced by this same community for a purpose. Identifying a genre is to make a generalisation. But for the most part, when we identify the genre of Old Testament texts this helps us to read it and to understand the testimony produced by the ancient community further.

GROUP QUESTIONS:

1. What is a 'genre'?

2. What differences exist between a poem and a story?

3. What are some of the challenges in identifying genres?

4. Read Psalm 42. Apply the 'tools of the trade' to this passage:

    i.   What is the significance to *them*?

    ii. What is the significance to *us*?

    iii. What is the significance to *me*?

RECOMMENDED READING

❧ Ryken, Leland, Wilhoit, James C. & Longman, Tremper III (eds) *Dictionary of Biblical Imagery*, (Downers Grove: IVP, 1998),

Although I have recommended many excellent resources, this one almost takes the cake as the ultimate resource. It is a dictionary that lists all the different images and concepts used in the bible and tracks where and how that image is presented. For example, it will list 'king' or 'shepherd' and discuss how that image/concept is understood in the culture and time of both the Old and New Testaments. It is particularly useful for preachers and songwriters.

⅍ Fee, G. D., & Stuart, D., *How to Read the Bible For all its Worth*, 3rd Ed., (Grand Rapids: Zondervan, 2003).

Although already recommended, when it comes to the study of genre this book is a must. It outlines in a comprehensive way the different genres found in the bible and how to read those genres appropriately.

ENDNOTES

1. Longman, T., *Making Sense of the Old Testament: Three Crucial Questions*, (Grand Rapids, Michigan: Baker, 1998), p. 40.

2. Charpentier, E., *How to Read the Bible: The Old and New Testaments*, (New York: Gramercy Books, 1981), p.25

3. Charpentier, E., *How to Read the Bible: The Old and New Testaments*, p.25.

4. Longman, T. , *Making Sense of the Old Testament: Three Crucial Questions*, p.41

5. Longman, T., *Making Sense of the Old Testament: Three Crucial Questions*, p.15.

6. Longman, T., *Making Sense of the Old Testament: Three Crucial Questions*, p. 16.

7. Birch, B.C., Brueggemann, W., Fretheim, T.E., & Petersen, D.L., *A Theological Introduction to the Old Testament*, 2nd Ed., (Nashville: Abingdon Press, 2005), p.283.

8. Brueggemann, W., 'Second Isaiah: An Evangelical Rereading of Communal Experience' in C. Seitz (ed) *Reading and Preaching the Book of Isaiah*, (Philadelphia: Fortress, 1988), p. 78.

Chapter 6

THE SIGNIFICANCE FOR *US*

By considering the purpose of the Old Testament for *them*, we are acknowledging that God speaks to people in a way that is real and relevant. God was active in the world of the ancient Israelites. The Old Testament is their testimony. It was written for them and by them. It is the record of God speaking in their world and about their world. God was speaking through their culture and language. But it has significance well beyond their time and place. Through the community and history of the Old Testament, God was working towards a plan. That plan was focused around the possibility of all humanity and creation being restored into relationship with God, not just the one community of ancient Israel. But this community of ancient Israel had a central part in this unfolding plan. It was through this group, identified as the 'people of God', that God was at work. It was from this community that Jesus Christ would come. Why does humanity need to be restored into relationship with God? Because of the fall of humanity into sin that is defined for us in the Old Testament (particularly Genesis 1-3). The New Testament relies on the Old Testament for this information that describes the reality of separation from God. Humanity has sinned and is in need of a saviour. In this sense, both the New Testament and the Old Testament are part of a bigger picture of God at work in the world. The testimony of ancient Israel has played an important part in this unfolding plan. Before we consider the significance of the Old Testament for *us*, let us review the testimony of ancient Israel that is so central to the coming of Jesus Christ.

Their testimony (or story) has been described as an epic. You may remember their story from the first chapter. Their testimony began with the creation of the world and the celebration of humanity as made in the 'image of God' (this will be further discussed in chapter 8). Their story then centred on one family, led by Abraham, and his descendants. According to the testimony of the biblical texts, this family sojourned in Egypt to avoid the fatality of famine. While living in Egypt they became slaves. But God did not forget them. God called his 'son' Israel out of Egypt (Ex 4:22; Hosea 11:1) through the waters of the Reed Sea to the desert. In the desert wilderness their covenant and status as 'God's people' was confirmed. However they were tested in the wilderness. The most crucial test of faith - to take possession of the land despite overwhelming opposition – they failed (Numbers 13-14). So they stayed in the desert for forty years. At the end of this period, they were led by Moses to the plains of Moab where they re-affirmed the law. This re-commitment to the law included new directions in how to live in the Promised Land. Under the leadership of Joshua, they took possession of the land through military force.

This testimony records that they settled in the Fertile Crescent and eventually (under their first stable king, David) established a united monarchy. However, this kingdom soon divided. They cycled from faith to unbelief and idolatry, back to faith then unbelief. Their testimony records that eventually, due to the rejection of their special covenant relationship with God, the two kingdoms fell. First the northern kingdom was taken by Assyria in 721 BCE.[1] Over a hundred years later, the southern kingdom (Judah) was captured by Babylon and taken into exile in 587 BCE. While the southern kingdom was in captivity, the Babylonians were overthrown by the Persians. After a period of time, the Persians (under King Cyrus) allowed the Judeans to return to their homeland to rebuild the city and Temple. They introduced many religious and social reforms but always struggled in their worship and political independence. Throughout these events as described in the biblical text, the community of faith continued to voice their prayers and praise to God in the various psalms and wisdom literature. This epic testimony of the older covenant 'people of God' is important for the Christian community to grasp in order to understand their identity and role as participants in the wider unfolding history of God's actions.

It was into this community of ancient Israel that God sent the saviour of the world. In the development of history and salvation which climaxed at the cross, Israel played a central role. As we have noted, Jesus was a part of a family and a nation that had a long history of dealings with God. This acknowledgement of the role of ancient Israel is where the New Testament begins. The first page of our New Testament (Matthew 1) begins with the genealogy of Jesus Christ. What does it tell us of Jesus? We are told in the very first verse that Jesus was the son of David and the son of Abraham. The New Testament begins by referring us back to the Old Testament story. It connects us with this older testimony in order to tell us about Jesus.[2] These two figures of Abraham and David were important people in the testimony of the Old Testament. But they are also important in the New Testament. They are important because they are part of the plan and wisdom of God that through this family of faith, Jesus Christ would be born.

By considering the purpose of the Old Testament for *us,* we are acknowledging that this plan of God did not end with ancient Israel but continued with the coming of Jesus Christ and the birth of the church. God continued to speak to people directly as the writings of the early church community highlight. The New Testament is the testimony of the early Church. It tells us of God speaking to and through this community. According to the testimony of the New Testament community, in the fullness of time, God sent his Son to save Israel and the nations. The testimony of ancient Israel has proved over and over again that they could not keep the law or save themselves. They needed a saviour. Jesus was (and continues to be) the answer. As Christian readers of the Old Testament, we bring this perspective to our reading. We acknowledge not only the significance of the passage for *them* (ancient Israel) but the significance of the passage for *us* (Christian readers). In considering this second perspective, it is like we are also reading the Old Testament with Christ-coloured glasses. Our perspective has changed with the knowledge of Jesus Christ so that we read our Old Testament with a new revelation and hope of God's plan. We read the beginning with the end in mind. We read the Old Testament (beginning) with knowledge of the New Testament (end). As we do this, it is important to acknowledge this process: we are reading backwards.[3] This is what makes our reading of the Old Testament uniquely Christian.

By reading backwards, we can see God's hand in the history and events of the Old Testament that directed the community to the point of readiness for the arrival of the saviour of the world. As we read backwards we can see hints and shadows of God's plan through Jesus Christ. However these were not obvious at the time, just as the true identity of a character in a mystery novel is not fully known or revealed until the end. But by reading backwards, we can see how these hints in the testimony point to the role and character of Jesus. Just as if you re-read the mystery novel you would see all the hints and signs to solving the crime that you missed the first time around. For example, we identify in Abraham's son, Isaac, something of the role of Jesus. Genesis 22 is a narrative. It tells a story of an event in the life of Abraham and his son Isaac. This story tells how Isaac was led by his father to a place of sacrifice. However as the story unfolds, it would not be a sacrifice of an animal that they would perform but the sacrifice of Isaac. Let us consider the significance of this passage firstly to *them* and then *us* as we 'read backwards'.

In Genesis 22, this son of promise was to be offered to God as a sign of Abraham's faith. It seems an unexpected request and contrary to both God's nature and ways. Although child sacrifice was a common practice among the people of the land of Canaan in which Abraham was living, this practice would later be illegal when the law was given at the exodus. The narrator does not tell us why God makes this request, we are only told Abraham's response: faith. With complete trust in God, Abraham leads the entourage to the place of sacrifice. Isaac carried the wood for his own sacrifice in obedience to his father. However just when the actual sacrifice is to be made, Abraham's hand is stayed. Isaac is safe. It was a test. It was a test of obedience which Abraham passed with flying colours. Instead, God provides an unblemished ram for their sacrifice and worship. God is revealed to be their provider (called 'Jehovah Jireh').

This story had significance to *them*. It was a testimony to the faith of Abraham and obedience of Isaac. It was a testimony to the faithfulness of God that the son of promise would be saved. From the lineage of Isaac, the nation of Israel would be formed. How is it significant to *us*? It is significant to *us* because from this family of Isaac, Jesus Christ would eventually come. But it is also significant because it gives us a hint or taste to what Jesus would be like. Jesus would be like the son who obediently carried the wood (in particular, the wood of the cross) for his own sacrifice. He is just like Isaac in his willingness to lay down his life for the love of his father. He is just like Isaac in that from the son a 'nation' would be born. However, the 'nation' birthed by Jesus Christ would not be a political or social group living in a specific geographic location. This nation birthed by Jesus would be a people group living in all different geographic locations from all different political and social backgrounds because they are a people of faith. This new kingdom established by Jesus is one of faith, not of ethnicity. The entry requirement is not birth into the Israelite family but faith (being 'born again'). When reading the Old Testament for *us*, we ask: Can I see Christ in this passage?

The Old Testament is crucial if we want to understand the role and work of Jesus. We see this principle throughout the New Testament. Who is Jesus? If someone stopped you in the street and asked you to describe Jesus, what would you say? You may respond with ready descriptions such as: He is the 'Son of God', the 'messiah', 'saviour', 'redeemer', the 'lamb of God who takes away the sin of the world', our 'High Priest', the 'Good Shepherd', and so the list continues. All these descriptions of Jesus Christ do not rest solely upon the witness of the New Testament. Most of these terms originate from the Old Testament. So to understand Jesus as the 'Son of God', 'redeemer' or our 'High Priest', we must look towards the Old Testament and not just the New Testament in isolation. By reading backwards, we can see hints and shadows of what our saviour Jesus would be like. The New Testament also notes many examples of this fore-shadowing or hinting in the Old Testament to Jesus and the new kingdom he would introduce.

However, by looking for Christ in an Old Testament text does not mean that every individual story, prophecy and event must point in some way to Jesus. As we read backwards we see lots of examples of this fore-shadowing, but also many examples where it is not found. While we see a fore-shadowing of Jesus in the person of Isaac in the story of Genesis 22, in the next chapter we do not see any such hints. In Genesis 23 we see Abraham bargaining for the purchase of a plot of land to be a burial place for his recently deceased wife, Sarah. This is actually the first time Abraham acquires some of the land he has been promised by God in Genesis 12-15. However, while it is significant as part of the fulfilment of the earlier promise given and full of cultural insights, there are not any obvious hints to Jesus in this story of Genesis 23. Therefore, we shouldn't force it or look for hints and shadows under the burial rocks. Yet, while this particular incident may not explicitly foreshadow Christ, we see that it is part of the 'big picture' which does point to Jesus. We can see how the testimony of this larger story of the Old Testament points to the life and ministry of Jesus. Christ fulfils the Old Testament scripture in the patterns of the overall story.

The book of Matthew in the New Testament tells of the birth of Jesus and the celebration of this baby as God in the flesh. Like the family of Abraham, the family of Jesus went to Egypt to avoid the fatality of this baby boy ordered by Herod (Matt 2). Similarly, out of Egypt the son was called (Matt 2:15). Jesus left Egypt and went through the waters of baptism where he was affirmed by the heavenly Father as the beloved Son (Matt 3:17). Their special relationship was confirmed. Matthew then tells us how Jesus was led into the wilderness where he was tempted and tested for forty days. While Israel had been unbelieving and rebellious in their forty year wilderness journey, Jesus was obedient. Jesus not only demonstrated faith but emerged victorious to go – like Israel – to the mountain to re-affirm the law. This re-affirmation of the law given by Jesus (beginning in Matt 5 with the Beattitudes) included new laws directing the people in how to live in the new 'Promised Land'. While Israel then took possession of the land through military force, Jesus was no less courageous. Emerging from the wilderness, Jesus was active in the spiritual realm taking possession of the new 'promised land' through healing, preaching, evangelism and the exorcism of demons. Where ancient Israel lacked faith and was an unfaithful son (like any of us have been), Jesus came as the faithful Son. By reading backwards, we can see how Jesus fulfils the larger pattern of ancient Israel's story established in the Old Testament. As we have noted already, the New Testament church lies in continuity with ancient Israel, not as a historical or familial extension, but through the reality of faith in Jesus Christ. We may not be direct descendents of Abraham or have his genes, but the New Testament tells us that if we have faith in God, then we are like spiritual descendants of Abraham (Rom 4:16).

Yet throughout this examination we have observed that while Jesus is the fulfilment of the Old Testament, life in this new covenant is not exactly the same. The new covenant of the New Testament is different to the older covenant of the Old Testament. When we talk about the Old Testament as being 'old', it doesn't mean that it should just be replaced by the 'new' (as for example an old model car is updated and traded in for a newer model). Instead, the Old Testament is vitally important for our Christian faith, but with the coming of Jesus Christ there has been a shift. There are continuities and dis-continuities between the two covenants.[4] In the New Testament, Christ inaugurated a new Kingdom. This new kingdom is not just a direct continuation of the testimony of ancient Israel but a transformation. So when we read the Old Testament as Christians we identify both a connection and a breaking with the older covenant. One of the best ways to see this shift or change is by looking at the important concept of the 'kingdom of God'.

The Old Testament presents a physical kingdom. The 'kingdom' was located in a physical, geographical place known as ancient Israel. That physical kingdom was established by military force under Joshua. It was defended and maintained against flesh and blood enemies. When the people disobeyed God and broke their covenant relationship they were physically removed from the land of this kingdom (in the exile). When they were restored, they were re-established in the physical, geographic domain of ancient Israel. The Old Testament ends with the expectation of a messiah who will come and save them from their enemies and establish a kingdom of peace centred in the Temple in Jerusalem. The Temple was regarded by the ancient Israelites as the physical location of God's dwelling place. It was this presence of God amongst them that set them apart from all the other nations. Even though by the time of Jesus there were other places of worship and teaching (such as the synagogues), the Temple was still the centre of worship. It was where the ancient Israelites would physically visit to demonstrate their devotion to God.

Within the sanctuary of the Temple, a copy of the law was kept. The law (or torah) was central to the life of the ancient Israelites. Particularly for Jews who were not physically near the Temple, they could express their devotion to God by their obedience to the law. By following the torah, the people were abiding by the way of life outlined by God. It was by following this 'guidance' and expected behaviour that Psalm 1 defines who is a righteous person. The laws were the rules of the 'kingdom'. In particular, the torah became focused on the practices of circumcision, keeping the Sabbath and the purity laws (to be discussed further in chapter 9).[5] By maintaining these practices, the ancient Israelites would demonstrate their dedication to God. The people who received and kept the torah were considered true Israelites. Yet being a true Israelite was not just a matter of keeping the law, but also a question of nationality. The people who comprised this covenant kingdom were from a particular socio-ethnic group living in the land. They were known as the ethnic group called 'ancient Israelites'. They identified their common ancestry from Abraham, Isaac and Jacob. To become a member of this kingdom community, you had to change nationalities. You had to become an ancient Israelite. Membership was made up of Jews only. To join them, non-Jews (or gentiles) had to convert. It is like they needed to have new citizenship that identified them as an ancient Israelite.

With the coming of Jesus, this kingdom and covenant is transformed. Jesus transforms this old kingdom to inaugurate a new kingdom. It is no longer a political, ethnic or geographic kingdom but a spiritual kingdom. In the Old Testament, God's people were a distinct political entity, the nation Israel. Today God does not work through a chosen nation, but a chosen people comprised from the nations of the world (Eph 2:15). The New Testament teaches a newer covenant in which the people of God do not obtain membership in the kingdom of God as a socio-political unit, but in the kingdom of God which is in the heart of believers. Now, it doesn't matter what country your passport says. If you are a follower of Jesus, you are part of his kingdom. You are part of the newly defined 'people of God.' We are an extension of the Old Testament 'people of God' not by our birth or ancestry, but by our faith. As Christians, we are not a people constituting a nation group, but are a people of faith living all across the world. Membership is now made up of Jews and Gentiles inclusive of all peoples from every tribe and tongue. The entry requirement is simple: faith in Jesus Christ.

Even the rules for the new kingdom have changed. The Old Testament prophet, Jeremiah, looked forward to the day when this new covenant would be formed. The new covenant that he saw would not be written on stone tablets like the torah. It would be written on the hearts of people (Jer 31:33). In the new kingdom established by Jesus, the torah that we follow is no longer about separating us as a distinct nation group. So we don't have to follow the particular laws of civil governance – because we don't need to live in the land of Israel to be people of God. Therefore, we are no longer required to practice the civil laws. If my bathroom has mould or mildew, I don't have to find a priest to inspect it to see how it needs to be cleansed. I follow the laws of the land that I live in. Similarly, the ceremonial laws of the sacrificial system are no longer applicable. Jesus died once, for all. So the practice of having to continually bring a blood sacrifice to restore my relationship with God is no longer required. Jesus has done it all (Hebrews 9). I now enter fellowship with God through faith in the Jesus Christ.

Yet what are we to do with Old Testament law? This is an important question that the New Testament believers wrestled with. They questioned how this new kingdom community should live. They also questioned what practices should mark them as 'true believers' in Christ. Should Christians still be circumcised following the practice of the Old Testament law? How should Christian behaviour be governed? In Matthew 22:37-40 we are given guidelines on how to live in this new kingdom. In this account, Jesus quotes from the Old Testament to define how we should live. We should love God with all our heart, soul and strength. It is a direct quote from Deuteronomy 6:6, which is part of the Torah. But what Jesus emphasises for us is a principle based on the higher law of love. This higher law continues to guide us in how we should live with one another. How should we live in community? Matthew continues: love your neighbours as yourselves. This is another direct quote from the torah, from Leviticus 19:18. We follow the higher order of love. But this is not a selfish, self-interested love. This is love defined by the cross – the ultimate act of self-giving and sacrifice demonstrated by Jesus. So we don't just abandon the law, but observe the principles of it. These principles are still upheld by the Ten Commandments (this issue will be discussed further in chapter 9). As Galatians 5:2 states: "For in Christ Jesus neither circumcision nor uncircumcision has any value. The only thing that counts is faith expressing itself through love" (TNIV). The principles of the law count, but the practice of the civil and ceremonial law is no longer required in this new kingdom.

Worship in the new kingdom established by Jesus is no longer a physical act. To show devotion, believers no longer have to travel to the Temple in Jerusalem. Worship is in spirit and truth (John 4:23). God's presence no longer just dwells in the Temple (the geographical location of Jerusalem) but in the heart of every believer. It is now the believer and the community of believers (1 Cor 3:16) that form the Temple in this new kingdom. It is in our fellowship and community, not in a physical construction, that the presence of God dwells. That is why believers can fellowship anywhere in the world – God is found in the unity of their fellowship, not in a building. Yet it is not only the place of worship that is radically transformed in this new kingdom, but the location of the kingdom as well.

Unlike Joshua who fought flesh and blood enemies to establish the kingdom for ancient Israel, Jesus began his ministry by fighting the spiritual powers at work in the world. Through preaching and healings, Jesus fought and established his kingdom. The climax of the new kingdom was at the cross and resurrection when Jesus triumphed over the enemy. Jesus triumphed over death, sin and the forces of darkness to win the fight (Col 2:13-15). As followers of Jesus Christ, we continue that work in the expansion of the Kingdom of God. Like Jesus, we do this through evangelism and spiritual warfare – not fighting against flesh and blood, but against the spiritual enemies of God (Eph 6:12). Because believers are now made up of Jews and Gentiles inclusive of all peoples from every tribe and tongue, there is no particular land or geographic location in this new kingdom that is more special than another. That is why there is no mention in the New Testament of a 'holy land', just a new 'holy people'.[6] However, this does not mean that this new kingdom is only 'spiritual'. We are not just spiritual people but are physical, emotional, and cognitive. We are holistic people living in a holistic world. The spiritual realm can impact the physical realm. In the same way, the physical realm can impact the spiritual realm. The salvation and new life found in Jesus Christ is not just a spiritual belief but must overflow into our daily practices, behaviour, social interaction and thought life.

Yet while we are no longer fighting a physical battle, it does not mean that texts like Joshua are no longer applicable. These testimonies from the Old Testament are not like the old appliance that no longer works so is completely replaced. Instead, they still tell us about how God acts in the world. They still provide a testimony of the ancient Israelites that we can learn from and apply. So, for example, our warfare in the New Testament is not physical but spiritual. There is a shift. Yet while the enemies of the new kingdom may not be located in the physical, geographic realm like the Old Testament, its testimony still has a lot to teach us. For example, in the midst of the physical warfare led by Joshua there are important principles of holiness that it can teach us, even though we do not practice the direct application of their physical warfare. So while there are dis-continuities between the older covenant and the newer covenant, we can still apply the Old Testament to this new situation. There is continuity of principles. To continue the example, our spiritual warfare still requires the faith demonstrated in the physical warfare of ancient Israel (even though some of the rules of the kingdom have changed). In all of this though, God is still the same.

So when we read the Old Testament as Christians we identify both a continuity and dis-continuity with the older covenant.

Some things continue the same, such as the faith demonstrated by Abraham and Joshua. Other things do not stay the same, such as the need to live in a specific geographic location. It is a great paradox that as Christians we define ourselves in complete solidarity as well as in radical dis-continuity with the testimony of ancient Israel. This is probably one of the most difficult aspects of reading the Old Testament as Christians. How do we know if a practice or concept is in continuity or dis-continuity with the Old Testament? How do we participate as the 'people of God' and identify ourselves in the on-going story of God in the world if the rules have changed? We look to the covenant of the new kingdom defined by Jesus. This is the principle of the cross.[7] Is the Old Testament event or practice in continuity or dis-continuity with the new Kingdom? We look to the cross. Jesus has laid down his life that we might find new life in him. So we follow the way of Christ. We act in faith and love. This means that as disciples of Christ, we follow after him and continue his mission. The victory is won, but the kingdom is not yet complete. This will only be resolved when Jesus establishes his full kingdom in time yet to come. So we continue the task of discipleship that Jesus has established. We continue to see this new kingdom of God renewed and expanded. Therefore, when reading the Old Testament for *us*, we ask: can I see us, as part of the ongoing Christian community, in this passage?

To demonstrate this, we will revisit our key text in the Old Testament of Genesis 12. In this passage, we have seen how a promise was given to Abraham that God would bless him, multiply him and through his seed all the nations of the earth would be blessed. We have also noted how this passage is significant to *them* (the Old Testament community) as it was the foundation of their identity as a nation and the 'people of God'. But we see with the coming of Christ, this passage takes on a whole new meaning as it becomes fulfilled in Christ. This passage is significant to *us*, as part of the New Testament community, because Christ is the promised seed and fulfilment of this promise. By reading backwards, we can see how this older covenant testimony of Abraham is fulfilled: that through the seed of Abraham (Jesus Christ) all the nations of the earth will be blessed. But it doesn't end there. According to Acts, the Christian community (or church) is also the continuation of this promise as we take this blessing of the good news to the nations. We also become the means of blessing. This mandate can also be seen as a continuation of the older covenant testimony of Abraham: that through the seed of Abraham (us, by faith) all the nations of the earth will be blessed (because we bring them the good news of Jesus). We are the continuation of that promise, through faith in Jesus Christ. This passage from the Old Testament is significant for *us* because we see how we (the Christian community) are also the fulfilment of this promise.

So as we read the Old Testament, we seek to understand the significance of the text to not only *them* (the ancient Israelites) but also to *us* (the Christian community). It is significant to us because by reading backwards with our Christ-coloured glasses, we can see not only Christ in the text but also how we continue the work of Christ to extend his kingdom in our world. Yet as members of the Christian community we also affirm that God speak to individuals. God speaks to *me* through Scripture. It is to this concern we next turn.

GROUP DISCUSSION QUESTIONS:

1. Who is *us*?

2. What is the difference between *me* and *us*?

3. What would happen if you didn't bother to consider the significance of a passage for *us*?

4. Read Isaiah 40:1-5. Apply the 'tools of the trade' to this passage:

    i. What is the significance to *them*?

    ii. What is the significance to *us*?

    iii. What is the significance to *me*?

RECOMMENDED READING:

ॐ Achtemeier, P. & Achtemeier, E., *The Old Testament Roots of our Faith*, (London: Abingdon, 1962)

This book is getting a bit old now, but it is still a valuable resource. It is easy to read and aimed at Christian readers of the Old Testament. It moves thematically through the bible to make connections between the two testaments.

ॐ Wright, N.T., *The New Testament and the People of God*, (SPCK, 1992)

This book is not for the faint-hearted! It is a academic book worth its weight in gold. This particular volume in the series analyses the origins of Christianity. It considers the historical context and expectations of Judaism that were revolutionised by the life and ministry of Jesus Christ.

ॐ Childs, B., *Biblical Theology of the Old and New Testaments*, (Minneapolis: Fortress Press, 1992)

Again, this is a more academic book. It tracks numerous concepts within the bible to see how the ideas develop from the Old Testament to the New and beyond.

ENDNOTES

1. BCE means 'before the common (or Christian) era'

2. Achtemeier, P. & Achtemeier, E., *The Old Testament Roots of our Faith*, (London: Abingdon, 1962), p.1

3. Brueggemann, W., *Theology of the Old Testament: Testimony, Dispute, Advocacy*, (Minneapolis: Fortress Press, 1997), p.732.

4. Longman, T., *Making Sense of the Old Testament: Three Crucial Questions*, (Grand Rapids, Michigan: Baker, 1998), p.84.

5. Wright, N.T., *The New Testament and the People of God*, (London: SPCK, 2002), p.230.

6. Wright, N.T., p.366.

7. Wright, N.T., p.367.

Chapter 7

THE SIGNIFICANCE FOR *ME*

In the first chapter, we questioned the different reasons why people read the Old Testament. For some, it is to gain knowledge of ancient cultures. For others, they read the Old Testament to see the hints of the life and ministry of Jesus Christ. For some people, it is to hear God's guidance in their daily lives. They listen for God's voice in and through the text. Maybe you are like me and you read it for all of the above reasons! Yet central to each of these responses is the idea that God speaks to people. God intervened in the lives of people in the ancient community of Israel. They wrote down that testimony of God's interactions and compiled their writings into the Old Testament we use today. Through their interaction with God we see how the world functions. We learn about ourselves. We understand who we were created by and what we were created for. We understand something of the nature of God's character through his interaction with ancient Israel. However, the New Testament tells us that the story did not end there. God intervened in history by the coming of Jesus Christ. The Christian community continues to read the Old Testament to gain insight into God's plan for the world. This means not only seeing these hints about Jesus' life, but also how God used a seemingly insignificant nation in the ancient Near East to reveal something of his own nature.

The early Church utilised the writings of the Old Testament in their own testimony (the New Testament) because God spoke to them through their pages. What is interesting to note is that the early Christian community did not take the Old Testament and 'cut and paste' sections from it that they liked and then throw out the rest. Sure they quoted the Old Testament a lot and referred back to it continually, but it was still kept as a unique testimony. They did not take it over. It was kept as a separate witness. They honoured the fact that this was the testimony of ancient Israel. They honoured the fact that it is the record of God's dealings with them. Although the New Testament community is a continuation of the plan of God established in the Old Testament, they kept it in its original form. God spoke to ancient Israel in direct communication through their culture and time. They recorded and preserved this testimony for us. God spoke to the New Testament church through these words of the Old Testament, as well as through direct communication in their culture and time. They also recorded and preserved this testimony for us. To read the text only for my personal devotion and development denies the relevance of God's message to the original community. The fundamental nature of the biblical witness is that God speaks to people where they are at.

From this perspective we can see that God speaks to us through the words of the Old Testament and New Testament, as well as through direct communication in our culture and time. So while we read the Old Testament honouring the significance for *them* (ancient Israel) and *us* (the Christian community), we also read it to hear God speaking to *me* as an individual believer. Because the time, culture, language, situation and circumstances of each believer is unique, God will speak a distinctive message to each person. God will speak to their individual situation in a way that is special to them. So if you speak Italian as your first language, then God will speak to you in Italian. Whether you are single, married, divorced or widowed, then God will speak to your specific situation. This does not say much about us, but is says a whole lot about God. God wants to speak and connect with you. God desires this so much it doesn't matter what language you speak or what culture you are in, God will come to you. God will meet you where you are at. Does this mean each of us should record and preserve every word we think

God might be saying for the benefit of future generations? Keep reading!

For many readers of the Old Testament, there is an expectation that God will speak to us through the text. There are many different ways that God does this. God can speak to us through the big events of the testimony of the Old Testament. Each encounter with God presented in the Old Testament can provide us with a pattern or testimony that we can learn from. For example, the exodus from Egypt can provide us with a pattern of leaving a place of slavery (such as sin or an old lifestyle) to a new life of hope. The Apostle Paul writes about some of these events in the Old Testament in 1 Corinthians 10:1-11. As he says in verse 5: "Now these things occurred as examples to keep us from setting our hearts on evil things as they did" (TNIV). In this sense, the testimony of the Old Testament was written for our benefit. It was written so we could learn from the mistakes and triumphs of ancient Israel in our own journey of faith. It was written so we can also learn something about God. Each pattern of the 'people of God' in this big picture of their testimony points us to the director of those events: God.

But it is not just the 'big picture' events that guide us in our life of faith. It is also the smaller events and individual stories that teach us about ourselves and God. We have noted some examples from the testimony of the Old Testament in our study already, including the story of Ruth. If you ever need to be reminded of God's hand in the normal occurrences of everyday life, then you will enjoy reading the book of Ruth. In this book there are no great miracles or deliverances or visions of God, yet God is very present. God is active in the life of a seemingly insignificant woman named Ruth. This story is set in the chaotic time of the Judges, after the Israelites have been delivered from Egypt and have settled in the land of Promise. In this story, an Israelite man called Elimelech takes his family to Moab because of a famine in the land. He leaves the land of Promise out of fear of starvation. But things get worse for this family. Although the sons marry Moabite women, all the men in the family soon die. This leaves Elimelech's wife, Naomi, and her two foreign daughters-in-law destitute. One of these daughters-in-law is named Ruth. Naomi hears that the famine has ended in Israel and decides to return to her homeland. She releases the girls from all responsibility in their culture to care for her. However Ruth refuses to abandon Naomi. She vows to return to Bethlehem with her. In a beautiful speech, Ruth deliberately revokes her own nationality and religion to embrace the worship of Naomi's God.

As the women return to Bethlehem, their situation is desperate. They are poor, homeless and without a 'father' to represent or care for them in this ancient culture. There was no social security in those days. Each family within the clan was required to care for their own widows and the poor. Yet, these unfortunate widows had no one. However the law given during the exodus provided a way for the poor and destitute to gain some food. The harvesters had to leave some of the grain in their fields to be collected by those without any income. So Ruth went to work. She happened to be harvesting in the field of a single, rich man named Boaz. He also happened to be in the same clan as Naomi. Boaz heard of Ruth and admires her dedication to her mother-in-law. He calls this foreign widow a 'woman of valour' like that also described in Proverbs 31. When Naomi hears of his attentions to Ruth, she hatches a plan. It is a daring and bold plan to secure the help of Boaz in providing familial protection and support for the women. The plan succeeds. Boaz acts on their behalf to bring them under the wing of his protection. He performs the cultural role of their kinsman-redeemer. It is a wonderful picture of God's care for his covenant people. There are many seeming coincidences in the story that point to the providential care of God. Boaz marries Ruth and they produce a son. This child would be the grandfather of David who would be the King of Israel. From this lineage of David, Jesus Christ would come. Boaz's actions even give us a hint of what Jesus Christ would be like in saving us and bringing us under his wing of protection. Jesus is our kinsman-redeemer.

The story of Ruth is a dramatic tale full of twists and turns. The story is also full of memorable and vivid characters.[1] In particular, the character of Ruth is a strong and courageous woman who is kind and patient. However her story is not a modern style biography. It is more like a character portrait. Her character portrait is given to help us navigate through life.[2] She provides an example of God's gracious provision and providential care. The story looks back to see what the characters could not see at the time: God at work. God's hand is only seen in hindsight. It provides an inspirational and encouraging example of God's secret work. Although we may not see God's hand in the visible realm of our lives or through miraculous events, God is working behind the scenes for those who fear him.

Ruth's story is a model of this truth that speaks to *me* today. For example, how do I respond when challenged by circumstances? When I feel forgotten by God? I think of Ruth. I remember God's faithfulness to her. I remember how God worked in secret. I remember that from this woman's family came the saviour of the world. I remember to look back on my life to see God's handiwork. Then I know I have not been forgotten. The story of Ruth helps to guide me in my Christian journey. It is like the story points to a particular universal truth or experience. The text acts as a sign that points to God's interaction with - and laws governing - the world. I can see through this story how God acts in the world. It points me to God. It inspires me to a new way of living and thinking. Yet that truth or sign cannot be divorced from the testimony in which it is presented. It is through this testimony of ancient Israel that God speaks to us. The story of Ruth not only tells me something about God, but it also speaks to my own life about situations and circumstances unique to me.

While we learn from the characters and events in the Old Testament, it does not mean that we have to copy their behaviour exactly. We learn from their life, but should not always mimic their actions. They lived in a different culture and a different time.

Sometimes the way Old Testament characters act is understandable in their own culture but would be inappropriate in our own. For example, it would be inappropriate for an unemployed or destitute person in our culture to pick the crops off someone's land just because that is what Ruth did. What was lawful in ancient Israel may not be lawful in our own context. Similarly, when Ruth takes action at Naomi's advice to secure the attention of Boaz, her ways are not exactly conventional (Ruth 3). Her unique method matched her unique situation. But we do learn the message of what Ruth's life demonstrates. God works in our lives to protect and provide for his covenant people. In the same way, many stories from the Old Testament teach us about God and about how to live. So when reading the Old Testament, we ask the question: what is the message of this text to *me*? How can I apply it to my unique context?

However, not all characters in the Old Testament are as noble and good as Ruth. Sometimes characters display both positive and negative qualities. They are, after all, only human just like us. We can learn from their mistakes. Other characters are models of behaviour we would *not* want to copy.[3] They are ruth-less! Although God worked in the situation of Naomi's family for good, we would not want to emulate their faithless departure from the land and place of God's promise. Elimelech's name means 'God is King', yet he did not act like he believed it. He did not act in faith. It is a challenging example, because each of us in times of difficulty like to solve problems in our own strength and in ways that seem practical to us. Yet the story does not condemn Elimelech. That is often the way with stories in the Old Testament – they just tell it as it was. The Old Testament doesn't always tell us explicitly whether a character was good or bad. This leads us to a difficulty: how do we know if a character is good or bad? We look at the fruit of their lives. We consider whether their actions produced faith and life, or doubt and death. The actions of Elimelech did not produce life and faith. We also judge the actions of Old Testament characters according to the measure given to them in that time. Generally this is in correspondence with the law. The ancient Israelites were given the law at the exodus. It defined how they should behave. It gave them the rules for living. If these characters acted contrary to the law, then their examples are warnings. Elimelech did not act in accordance with the law that promised God's faithfulness to his covenant in providing people with crops and fruitfulness (Deut 28) if they trusted and obeyed. He reaped the consequences of living in opposition to the covenant. Yet, despite Elimelech's unfaithfulness, God proved faithful in the end by providing for the widowed women. God did not forget them.

Yet it is not just the stories and law of the Old Testament that speak to each of us today. The wisdom writings of the ancient community also provide valuable insights and guidance for living. The practical sayings of the Proverbs delightfully encapsulate some of the wisdom of ancient Israel. They particularly give insight in how to negotiate social interactions. It is almost like a manual of personal development. They help guide us through life.[4] The book of Proverbs is balanced by the dialogue of Ecclesiastes and Job that question some of the bigger issues in life. These writings remind us that the life of faith is not just about personal development but about our moral fibre and character. Our attitude and conduct is meant to reflect the attitude and conduct of our creator God. Similarly the poetry of the Psalms continues to speak to us today. They are the prayers and thanksgiving of ancient Israel. They speak to us in their raw honesty and teach us also to be honest with God. Yet in the midst of their rawness, the Psalms guide us to the place of faith. They remind us of the centrality of worship to this pilgrimage we share in common. They model worship for us. Each of these types of writings (genres) are preserved to inspire us in our life of obedience and faith. They are not just artefacts of the past, but can speak with a freshness and vitality to each of us today.

If the testimony of the Old Testament speaks to us today, how does it work? How does it speak to us personally in this fresh and vital way? As we have noted, we can learn from the bible through its examples and teachings that guide us in life. They reveal something about God and ourselves. But sometimes a passage will seem to jump off the page and even slap you in the face! Sometimes it is a passage that you have read before, but suddenly it seems alive and fresh. Something in your heart tells you that it is a special message for you. This process of reading is often described as a 'rhema'[5] word or as the 'aha' moment of revelation. While the term 'rhema' itself is not quite accurate, it is an attempt to describe the sense that the text is speaking directly to the reader. It represents the moment of understanding spiritual truths. The Holy Spirit illuminates a truth or concept from the reading or study of the biblical text. Probably a better term to refer to this experience of revelation is the Hebrew term 'yada' which means "to know".[6] However 'yada' is not just about knowledge of the mind but an experiential knowledge of the whole being. It involves the heart. It is the same word used in the Old Testament to euphemistically refer to the intimacy of sexual relations. But generally, it means to have an experiential knowledge that engages the heart and mind.

When reading the Old Testament, the 'yada experience' is this moment of new insight and understanding. It is the discovering of new insights into God, the world or ourselves. It is like a veil has been lifted from our eyes; the text which was obscured and dulled before is now seen in a new light. There is a sense of intimacy and appreciation in this 'yada experience' as the passage becomes a part of us. God speaks to us today through the Old Testament. Therefore it is important that we read the bible with an open heart and mind, and trust the Holy Spirit to speak directly from Scripture into our lives. It is an opportunity to encounter God in the reading experience. The significance of the biblical text to the individual reader – *me* – is a crucial element of this reading model. As we approach the Old Testament with the goal of hearing from God, we need to ask the significance of the words for *me*?

Yet, this 'yada experience' is not something we necessarily manufacture on our own. It reminds us that God speaks to us as unique individuals. The unique situation and context of the reader is addressed through the voice of the Spirit. The Spirit speaks to the reader through the bible. The same God that inspired the message of the bible continues to speak to us through those words. This role of the Holy Spirit is crucial for us as we seek to hear God's voice and guidance through the Old Testament. Just as God spoke to the ancient Israelites and the New Testament community, God wants to speak to me and you today. The 'yada experience' is a gift from God for the purpose of knowing God. While God may speak to you separate to the reading of the bible, Scripture is the authoritative means by which God has chosen to reveal himself. While God may speak to me, the bible is the measure that I use to evaluate the message I have heard. It is the measuring stick (remembering our discussion on the 'canon' in chapter 2) by which I can assess this 'revelation'. While I may record these insights for my own benefit, they are not necessarily authoritative for the whole Christian community per se.

So how do you know if it is God speaking or just your own thoughts? This is a very serious question. In every personal reading of the bible there is a potential for what is called idolatry. This is where we give an idea, concept or image a higher authority than God. While the ancient Israelites often struggled against worshipping idols and carved statues, we often struggle against worshipping ideas or concepts. This includes relying on our own strength and resources rather than God. Yet idolatry can occur when we are reading the bible. This idolatry occurs when we project our own interests, desires, and selfhood onto the message which the biblical text proclaims. When I do this, I am reading my own thoughts and ideas into the text. For example, if I have an idea that it is permissible to take fruit and crops from someone else's garden then I might read the book of Ruth and say that it is acceptable for me to take someone's fruit because Ruth did it. I have just gone to the bible to justify my pre-existing thought. Or, perhaps more seriously, if I am dating a lovely

non-Christian man I might think that it is permissible to marry
him even though he is outside of the Christian community because
Ruth was from a different religion when she married Naomi's son.
In doing this I am immediately transposing the testimony of Ruth
onto my situation. I do this because it matches what I want, not
because the bible as a whole teaches this. In this case, the bible no
longer acts as an independent authority. It no longer challenges me
with prophetic integrity but simply mirrors my own assumptions
or misassumptions. By reading this way, we can unsuspectingly re-
create the text (and God) in our own image.[7] We are then using a
bible passages to justify our own ideas, concepts and theology. And
while there is always grace in each of these examples, it may not be
what the text is trying to tell you! This is why we need to question
ourselves. We need to challenge our self-interests and motives.

So (back to our question) how do you know if it is God
speaking or just your own thoughts? How do we avoid this idolatry?
We can avoid this by reading the Old Testament in continual
reference to the significance of the passage to *them* and *us* as well as
me. By reading this way, I am measuring this 'revelation' against the
bible in its totality. I am reading the Old Testament passage through
the filter of my Christian faith as well as the faith of ancient Israel.
If the thought in question is consistent in its theology and fruit,
then we can feel pretty secure that it is a God-inspired thought.
Sometimes this takes time to reflect on the revelation - especially if
we are unsure. Time will tell. Your particular revelation may be like
the manna-bread in exodus that feeds us for the day but becomes
mouldy and 'off' by the next (Exodus 16). That's why even if we
don't have a 'yada experience' every time we read the bible, it is still
crucial that we are reading it. As I read the bible for the significance
for *them*, *us* and *me*, I am learning the bible in its entirety. If I only
read some passages, or only ask the significance of the passage for *us*,
then I am only seeing part of the picture. It is like only knowing one
or two characteristics of an acquaintance. But when we know a good
friend, we know the fullness and complexities of their personality.

Accordingly, by being faithful, daily readers we are absorbing the testimonies, concepts and theology of the bible that form this full and intricate picture of God at work in the world. Each part of this reading model must be heard for its unique contribution. The role of *them, us* and *me* functions as balancing factors in the reading process. Yet, we should always be sharing these thoughts with other people. Sharing our revelation within the security of Christian fellowship helps us to determine whether a revelation is from God or is our own self-interest. We help each other, even when it means challenging the idolatry in our readings.

However, it does not end here. The 'yada experience' should represent more than just the fresh understanding of a particular truth or insight. We must be changed by the experience. To use an example from James, this would be like seeing our faces in a mirror and then walking away and forgetting what we look like (James 1:23-24). We must apply and live the revelation we have received. God does not speak to us so that we can just be the same. When God speaks to us, our world is changed. This includes not only positive affirmation, but also the challenge to do better. The biblical text might be challenging you to a new way of living or thinking. With the revelation comes responsibility. The result of our 'yada experience' should be transformation. This involves the reshaping of our world-view and identity. It is like this friend that we know so well suddenly reveals something that we did not know before. Just say, for example, they reveal that they are allergic to peanuts. With this revelation comes responsibility. As a committed friend, my behaviour must be altered. When we go to dinner or meet for coffee, I will not attempt to feed them my special peanut cookies. I will change my behaviour with the revelation of this new knowledge. In the same way, when God's word reveals a fresh challenge to our character or behaviour, we must be willing to embrace the change. If I read in the book of Ruth that God works in hidden ways to protect and provide for his covenant people, then I need to make sure that I am a living example of this truth. When circumstances look sour or a crisis comes, I am challenged to trust God to work in the unseen as well as the seen realms as I am faithful and obedient to this Christian walk. Thus, the significance of the text for *me* also involves the purpose of shaping Christian identity and behaviour.

When we read the bible, we read it to know God better. Through it, we allow God to speak into our life. So this question also addresses the meaningfulness and message of the biblical text to you as the individual reader. It questions what God is saying to you personally through this passage or concept that is specific to your life and unique to where you're at right now. But it is important that in doing this step that we put some guidelines in place – that is, we keep in mind what the text means to *them* and *us*. As I live in faithful response to the revelation knowledge from Scripture, I participate as part of the ongoing 'people of God'. The reading of the text by *me* must be part of the bigger story; the story of God's interaction with the people of faith from all generations. I continue in the lineage of the people of faith who lived, recorded and preserved the testimonies in our bible. This reminds me that I do not read alone. Although I want to know God's direction and voice for my specific situation, I am not the only person in the world! I am part of the wider Christian community, sometimes referred to as the 'body of Christ'. We are individual readers who corporately form a reading community. We are not isolated readers, but part of the Christian community.

This means that the reading of Scripture is both a personal and public matter. The significance of the text to *me* is a private question. The significance of the text to *me* is determined according to the identity and context of *me*. The message and 'yada experience' will be different for each reader. It is a personal message from the biblical text specific to my situation. However, each *me* (or reader) is located in a community of readers. This makes the outcome and application of reading a public issue as they live and act in a wider community. You are not just a private reader because you live and act in a community.

This aspect of reading the bible is often overlooked and undervalued. Our societies in the Western world are usually very individualistic. We think that revelation is only for our personal benefit. However, the bible was written for more than just our personal significance. Just as a body requires the blood to be shared, so does the body of Christ require the insight and 'yada experience' of its participants to be shared. It is not just private knowledge. This not only helps others to be blessed by the revelation you have received, but also helps you to evaluate and measure your insight against the accumulated knowledge of God's word. It is this same Christian community that we also invite others join. The Christian community identifies with the evangelistic mandate given to the ancient Israelite community to proclaim God's character and salvation to those who do not know God (see, for example, Isaiah 60: 1-5). The mandate of *them* continues through *us* and *me* to reach the 'other'. Our faith is not just personal. It requires us to demonstrate the gracious character of our creator God through our public and private worlds to those yet to know him.

This discussion of the personal significance of the reading the text concludes this first section of the book. In Part I, you have now been equipped with the tools for reading the Old Testament. These tools have been summarised by three strategic questions:

1. What is the significance of this passage for *them*?
2. What is the significance of this passage for *us*?
3. What is the significance of this passage for *me*?

We are now ready to apply these tools to the 'big picture' of the Old Testament in Part II. This section will present some of the major events and concepts in the testimony of ancient Israel as presented in the Old Testament. We will also examine specific texts to see how our tools can be applied to different types of passages. The outline of the basic content of the Old Testament will then provide you with the framework to explore specific individual passages. It is to this 'big picture' we now look.

Group Discussion Questions:

1. Who is *me*?

2. What would happen if you didn't bother to consider the significance of a passage for *me*?

3. What are some of the potential problems in reading the passage for *me*?

4. Read Isaiah 6: 1-13. Apply the 'tools of the trade' to this passage:

    i.   What is the significance to *them*?

    ii. What is the significance to *us*?

    iii. What is the significance to *me*?

Recommended Reading

❧ Peterson, Eugene H., *Eat this Book: The Art of Spiritual Reading*, (London: Hodder & Stoughton, 2006).

This is refreshing book that is quite poetic in its expression. As you would expect from Eugene Peterson, it is an imaginative reflection of the purpose and action of spiritual reading.

❧ Foster, Richard, *Celebration of Discipline* (London: Hodder & Stoughton, 1980)

I recommend this book not so much for its study on how to read the bible, but on its introduction to the spiritual disciplines of the Christian life. It provides an excellent and practical outline of these practices such as prayer, fasting, etc. Highly recommended.

ENDNOTES

1. Longman, T., *Making Sense of the Old Testament: Three Crucial Questions,* (Grand Rapids, Michigan: Baker, 1998), p.14.

2. Longman, T., *Making Sense of the Old Testament: Three Crucial Questions,* p.14.

3. Longman, T. *Making Sense of the Old Testament: Three Crucial Questions,* p.14.

4. Longman, T., *Making Sense of the Old Testament: Three Crucial Questions,* p.17.

5. It is a term based on a Greek word (*rhema*) that is an immediate or personal word as opposed to another Greek word, "logos", that is a general or distant word. However, unfortunately this differentiation is not a correct understanding of the Greek words. This issue is discussed by Matthew Clark in his doctoral thesis: 'An Investigation into the Nature of a Viable Pentecostal Hermeneutic', Thesis for D Th, Pretoria: Unisa, 1997, p.68.

6. Bridges-Johns, Cheryl, & Johns, Jackie D., (1992) 'Yielding to the Spirit: A Pentecostal Approach to Group Bible Study,' *Journal of Pentecostal Theology,* Vol 1, p 112.

7. Thistleton, Anthony, *New Horizons in Hermeneutics,* (Grand Rapids: Zondervan, 1992) p.530.

Part II:

Applying the Tools

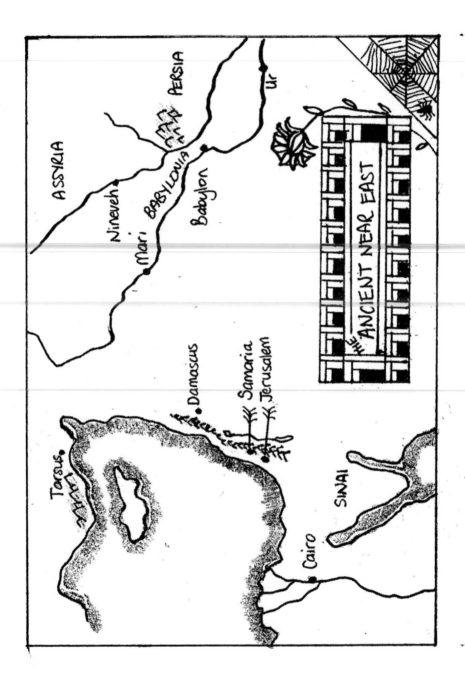

THE ANCIENT NEAR EAST

Chapter 8

FROM CREATION TO ABRAHAM

In our journey so far, we have learnt some of the tools of the trade. These tools equip us in *how* to read. What this next section in the journey aims to uncover is *what* we are reading in the Old Testament. In Part II we are outlining the 'big picture' of this testimony of ancient Israel. Beginning with creation and moving through the major events and concepts, it will create a picture of their story. It is like we are building a house. This outline provides the scaffolding in which the house can be built. It is not a detailed description of the house. It is more of a sketch of the frame. However it provides a foundation from which you can keep building the house. In the same way, this is not a detailed examination of the testimony of ancient Israel. It is an overview. Hopefully, between the tools and scaffolding provided, you will feel confident enough to keep reading on your own. This sets you up for a life-long journey of reading the Old Testament. It is not a makeshift house, but a long-term project!

The Old Testament begins with the book of Genesis. As its name suggests, it is a book of beginnings. It is a compilation of the testimonies of ancient Israel about their origins. As we open its pages we are immediately confronted with the power and sovereignty of God. This God of ancient Israel is the creator of the universe. He spoke it into being and holds it in place. This world was created for a purpose. That purpose was to shine and reflect the majesty of the creator. These opening chapters portray God in relationship with his creation on a wide scale. The testimony then narrows down to a particular family. Structurally, the book of Genesis falls into two distinct sections. The first eleven chapters are known as the 'primeval history'. This means that it contains the really ancient accounts. They are the stories of origins.

This primeval history begins with creation then traces the unfortunate downward spiral of the human race. It follows their fall into sin to the two climactic judgements of God - the flood and the dispersal after the building of the Tower of Babel. The next section (from chapter 12 to 50) focuses on one family, led by Abraham. This is referred to as the 'patriarchal history'. Out of all humanity at that time, God chose to reveal himself through interaction with one family. Why this family? It was an act of God's grace. There was nothing inherently special about Abraham or his family. The narrative simply presents God's gracious selection and their obedient response. This patriarchal history also presents a story of origins. It is from this family that the nation of ancient Israel would come. The rest of the Old Testament tracks the testimony of this family and nation established by Abraham. As the New Testament reminds us, it is from this nation and family that Jesus Christ would eventually be born. However, as a very musical Austrian novice called Maria once said, we must start at the very beginning.[1]

The first pages of the bible introduce us to the creator of the world. They establish right from the beginning that Yahweh – the Hebrew name for God used in the Old Testament –is the creator and the one to whom all of creation is accountable. It doesn't tell us how God came into existence. God is pre-existent. He is a constant. The pre-existent God brought everything that exists into being. Until God spoke, nothing existed. The created order emerged in obedient response to the articulated will of the Creator. In the cultural context of polytheism (worship of many gods), this statement was revolutionary. It was like ancient Israel was drawing a line in the sand and affirming that it was not the gods of Egypt or Babylon that formed the world. These other nations also had their stories of origins (this category of stories are technically called a 'myth' which is different to our modern understanding of 'mythology'). However, the book of Genesis makes it very clear that the creator of the world was Yahweh.

Genesis presents us with two separate but complementary narratives that tell us of the creation of the world. These are commonly identified as Genesis 1 (1:1- 2:3) and Genesis 2 (2:4 – 2:25). They have a slightly different purpose in that Genesis 1 gives us the bigger outline. In this account, God is ultimate and sovereign. In comparison, Genesis 2 presents a more intimate account of the relationship between God and people. God is more like a concerned parent who looks out for the health and needs of their children. These accounts were not written as a science manual or for the purpose of defending a specific scientific theory; they are a narrative. Yet, while both of these accounts are identified as using the genre of narrative, Genesis 1 is more of a poetic narrative. It is much more structured and uses lots of repetitions. It presents the creation as deliberate, thoughtful and highly structured.

The creation account of Genesis 1 follows a pattern. One of the exercises in the study questions at the end of this chapter is for you to draw this pattern as a table diagram. You might like to try it now. This pattern is introduced in the second verse of Genesis chapter 1 where it tells us that the earth was "formless and empty". In Genesis 1, God gives form to creation and then fills it. In the first three days, the form or foundation is established. This form is then filled in the following three days. So on day 1, God created light in general (the form). On day 4, he created specific kinds of light (the sun, moon and stars) that filled the form previously prepared. On day 2, the sea and sky (the form) were created. On day 5 they are filled with the creatures of sea and sky. On day 3, God created the dry ground. On day 6, he made the creatures of land to fill the dry ground. The climax to creation is the seventh day. This is the day of rest for God. However, this was not a permanent holiday. The bible continually reminds us that God is still active in his creation. He continues to care for his handiwork.

This poetic narrative is important because it tells us many things. Primarily, it tells us about God. In a narrative or story, characters are known by their description, speech and actions. In this creation narrative, we are not given much description of God. However we are told plenty about the actions of God. In fact, God is the primary actor who creates the universe by his words. It presents God as completely sovereign. God speaks, and all of nature - everything that exists - obeys. The whole process is very structured and ordered. This also tells us something about God. The process of creating the form in three days that is then filled in the following three days indicates completeness and wholeness. This account also tells us a lot about humanity. Humanity is a special act of God's creation. They are not just one of the animals. They reflect some of the intelligence and creativity of God. Humanity is unique because we are made in the image and likeness of God. In Genesis 1:26, a pronouncement is made by God. It is presented like a royal decree: "Let us make human beings in our image, in our likeness" (TNIV).

This concept is extremely important in the theology of the Old Testament. Humanity is made in the image and likeness of God. Yet, what does this mean? In Babylonian accounts, which we noted in chapter 4, we saw they credited Marduk with the creation of the earth. In their writings (the Enuma Elish), the creation of the earth is the result of a fight between some of their gods. Humanity was formed to do the work that the gods didn't want to do. In this story, the creation of humanity is an after-thought. The gods are not noble or good, but petty and selfish.[2] In comparison, the Old Testament presents the creation of humanity as a special and deliberate act of God. They are infused with dignity. God is like a sovereign king who creates with purpose and thoughtfulness. Humanity is made in the image of that king to be stewards of the earth. Our purpose is a noble one - to mirror God to the world and creation.

The use of the plural 'us' in this royal decree by God is understood by many theologians to be a reference to the trinitarian nature of God. The concept of the Trinity is probably one of the hardest doctrines of the bible to grasp! However what this statement in Genesis 1:26 highlights is that God is a relational being. It highlights the essential nature of God – Father, Son and Spirit – as being a community. This means that God is fundamentally a relational being. You can't have a son without a father. Similarly, you need to have a father to have son. The Spirit is sometimes understood as the bond of love between them.[3] As God speaks the word in creation, the Spirit acts (Gen 1:2). The creator God is an interactive, relational and communicative being. As this decree continues, it reminds us that both female and male are made in the image of this God. So if we are made in the image and likeness of God, then our essential nature is also to be interactive, relational and communicative beings. To be made in the image of God is to belong in community. The image of God resides not simply in the individual human being but in the community of humankind. However, while we are made in the image of God, this Genesis account is very clear that we are not God. We are both like God (made in God's image) and different from God.[4] We are the creation and not the creator. We are created to interact not only with God and each other, but also with the rest of creation.

Part of the role appointed to humanity is to care for the rest of creation. We have a responsibility to steward this creation of God. We represent God to the rest of creation. We are like little kings appointed by the ultimate sovereign king. This highlights another implication of this idea of being made in the image of God when understood in its cultural context. In the ancient Near East, kings and royalty were perceived to be descended from the gods. They were also thought to have attributes and functions like the gods. Being descended from these divine beings, the kings were said to be made in the image and likeness of their gods. For this reason, it was only the origins and genealogies of kings that were recorded in their sacred writings because they were the special ones. But here in Genesis, it is not just a special class of people that are made in God's image but all of humanity. All people are special and are worthy of this royal status and dignity. This ideology overflows into the whole Old Testament as the genealogies of all the families of ancient Israel are recorded (not just the kings) because all people are special. All humanity is commissioned with the task of stewardship. As we work together, in community, to fulfil this task of stewardship we are not alone. We are created to work together. Of course, the final aspect of this royal decree is the task of reproduction and multiplication. This definitely involves working together! It is part of the blessing of the creator upon creation.

For *us* as Christian readers, this account establishes God's intention for humanity. It is an intention that has been thwarted by the choice of humanity to reject God's rulership and relationship. As Philippians 2:6-8 reminds us, humankind has exploited this image of God by grasping at equality with God. But Jesus Christ did not exploit this image or his equality with God. In humility and obedience, Jesus took on human likeness in God's service. Through Jesus Christ, relationship with God can now be restored and that image can now be renewed (2 Cor 5:17; Col 3:9-10).

Take a moment to consider the significance of this concept of the image of God using our tools of the trade. How is this passage significant to *them, us & me*? The significance might be demonstrated by the following illustration. It is my personal attempt to symbolically represent the message of Genesis 1:27. While I make no claim to excellence in graphic art, it is an attempt to capture (through a drawing) the significance of this verse for *them, us & me*.

The significance to *them* is:

- Humanity is a special act of God's creation

- They are made by royal decree. This highlights the dignity and nobility of humanity (*see the crown above the oval mirror*)

- Humanity is part of creation and integrally linked to the world through their role as steward and royal representative of God (*the mirror is part of the creation of the trees*)

- Humanity mirrors the nature and character of God to creation (*the woman and man are within the oval mirror*)

The significance to us is:

- This special relationship to God has been severed by the sin and independence of humanity from our Creator. Jesus came to restore that relationship. He provides the bridge that restores fallen humanity to the fullness of this original purpose (*bridge that crosses the river of divide*)

- Jesus Christ is the ultimate representation of the image of God. By taking on human form, the life of Jesus reflects the fullness of what this image should look like (*he is the star in the centre of the mirror*)

Although this will be different for each reader, **the significance to *me* is**:

- The triune nature of God is reflected our relational nature. We are created for community (*sun with three rays*)

- Both male and female are made in this image (*both a woman and a man are represented*). As a woman, I reflect the majesty and dignity of God. But I do not just do this alone as an individual. It is in community that I reflect this image of God

- We all reflect different aspects of God, including the creativity of God (*as represented by the very attempt to illustrate this concept!*)

Yet, if Jesus Christ came to restore relationship between God and humanity, how has humanity rejected God? The origins of this alienation from God are outlined in the second creation narrative of Genesis 2. As we have noted, Genesis 2 presents God more as a concerned parent than awesome king. God shows care and provision for the intimate needs of all of creation. The narrative begins with the need of the earth for a carer. So from the earth (the Hebrew word is *adamah*), God creates the man (*adam*). Yet this situation is not satisfactory because God notices that the man is alone. God acts to provide a solution to this problem of aloneness. So from the man (now called in the Hebrew *ish*), God creates the woman (*ishah*). As a helper, she is not inferior or superior but comparable.[5]   Eve was not given to serve Adam, but to serve *with* him. She is not identical to him, but is an equal who complements him as a perfectly fitted partner. However, the plot thickens.

Within this seemingly harmonious situation, a conflict emerges. This is a common feature of narratives (or stories) - there is always a complication to the plot. In this narrative, the authority and rationale of their God-parent is questioned. While God had given the couple permission to eat from any of the trees in the garden except for one, they are tempted by what they cannot have. They not only doubt God's commandments, but doubt his integrity. They declare autonomy from God in a blatant act of disobedience. They eat from the forbidden tree. This first couple rebelled against its creator and broke their relationship with God. The result of their disobedience is alienation and separation. According to Genesis 3:8-24, they are changed by the act of the eating. They are charged with disobedience and punished in what is known as the 'Fall of Humanity'. The result of their disobedience is a curse. Alienation and pain is introduced into each of their situations. For example, the bond between the *ish* and *ishah* is altered. They will be competitors rather than complementary. The bond between the *adam* and *adamah* is altered. The man's service is changed to hard labour. Yet the essential dignity of humanity is not totally lost (Gen.9:6). They are still in the image of God after the fall. The image of God is seen clearly in Christ, and is restored to us fully in Christ (Rom.8:29).

Yet, the theme of creation does not just end with Genesis 3. It is a central idea throughout the Old Testament and entire bible. It is based on the premise that God is creator. God has defeated the idols and false gods, and so deserves our worship. This creator God has a plan for the world in which ancient Israel is a key player. The Old Testament looks forward to when this plan will incorporate the Gentiles (i.e. non Jews). This is fulfilled in the New Testament. This is the hope that all the nations will come to realise what ancient Israel and creation already know – that Yahweh is God. When this salvation comes to its fullness, the Old Testament looks forward to a reversing of this curse so that even creation will return to its original intention. The future redemption of humanity is implied in Genesis 3:15. It speaks of the seed of the woman crushing the head of the serpent (often identified as a satanic figure). This is fulfilled in Christ (Heb.2:14-15; Rom.16:20).

The book of Genesis commences on a cosmic scale. While humanity is made in the image of God, it is soon clear that they need a saviour. The Old Testament then follows this concern for restoration. While humanity declines in their self-centeredness and rebellion through the Flood and tower of Babel events (or testimonies), God never gives up on his creation. To provide redemption for humanity, the biblical testimony begins to focus on one family. This family from Mesopotamia are led by Abraham (originally Abram but is later changed to Abraham). However, in Genesis 12 Abraham is called and led by God to leave his ancestral home. As we noted in chapter 1, he is called to break from his corrupted community to lay the foundations for a new community. This will be the means of redemption. Abraham is promised descendants and a special land for these descendants. They become the focus of God's redemptive plan through the institution known as 'covenant'.

Covenant is an important theme within the Old Testament. The bible itself points to its centrality. The word 'testament' means covenant. So when we talk about the Old Testament and New Testament, we are talking about the Old Covenant and the New Covenant. It is a concept that unifies the bible. The old covenant is fulfilled by Jesus Christ to make the new covenant. Essentially a covenant is an agreement. It is a legally binding agreement between two parties. These two parties form a specific relationship with certain loyalties and obligations to which they must adhere. These obligations usually include conditions of behaviour. A modern day example of a covenant is marriage. Two parties agree to live together in physical, emotional and social union. They pledge to be loyal to each other and forsake all other potential partners. They are obligated to be loyal and true, even in the face of hardship. In general, while covenants have an initial formation, both parties are required to commit to the ongoing health and sustenance of the relationship. If they fail to live up to these expectations, there are certain consequences and possible punishments (depending on the nature of the agreement).

In the ancient Near East, animals were often sacrificed as part of the covenant ceremony. The death of the animal represented the fate of the covenant party if they failed to meet their obligations. This was culturally specific to ancient communities and is not recommended for a contemporary wedding ceremony! However this ancient custom does reflect the inherent nature of the concept, as covenant literally means "to cut". For example, if this agreement was a military treaty, then the consequences for failure of covenant obligations would be military annihilation. The agreement could not be altered except by the consent of both parties. This reminds us that covenant is essentially a relationship. It is about the formation of a relationship and the ongoing maintenance of that relationship. In the Old Testament, the covenant ceremony often concluded with a meal. The sharing of a meal represented fellowship between the parties involved.

The most common type of covenant relationship referred to in the writings of the ancient Near East was probably the political treaty.[6] Archaeologists over the last century have uncovered libraries, particularly across Mesopotamia, with numerous legal documents outlining political covenants. The most common type was what is called the 'vassal-suzerain treaty'.[7] This was an alliance between two unequal parties – the greater king (suzerain) and the lesser king (vassal). The vassal-suzerain treaties were often used to create relationships between nations or people groups, usually when one nation was conquered by another. It is the imposition of the powerful king upon that of a lesser king.[8] Because the suzerain has conquered the vassal, they owed their very life to this powerful king. The vassal could have been annihilated, but the suzerain has chosen to save them. So the vassal owes them their life and allegiance. The treaty or covenant outlines this relationship. It usually had a specific structure that included the demands, obligations and obedience expected of the relationship. The suzerain would offer their ongoing grace and protection to the vassal in exchange for their loyalty, support and tribute (protection money). The vassal was expected to be faithful to their suzerain. They pledged their exclusive loyalty. This meant the vassal could not engage in any other relationships or treaties without the consent of their suzerain. If they did, they were guilty of treason, and subject to the death penalty. The curses and penalties of the covenant would then come upon them. Entering into a treaty agreement was often the only choice for many people groups (including ancient Israel) who were caught between larger powers, as it offered them a means of security in troubled times.

While many of the covenants between ancient Israel and God are not identical to these vassal-suzerain treaties, it does help us to understand the concept. At the heart of the biblical covenant is the concept that God has saved Israel. God has rescued them. Therefore they owed their allegiance and very life to God. Yahweh is like the powerful King who enters into relationship with ancient Israel, his vassals. God is bound by treaty to his people. God used a human legal convention (the treaty) to reveal himself to his people. However, the vassal-suzerain treaty is not the only type of covenant in the bible or ancient Near East. Other examples of covenant agreements in the Old Testament include military alliances, marriage relationships and friendship pacts (such as Genesis 14). The use of covenant in the Old Testament focuses primarily on the covenant between God and humankind. What is interesting about 'covenant' is that it is a concept woven into the narrative. There is no real 'theological discussion' of covenant or definition given. In fact it was so common to the culture of the ancient Near East that it would have been assumed knowledge. However, the concept is continually implicitly used in the Old Testament through their stories and testimony.

One of the most significant covenants in the Old Testament is introduced in the narrative of Genesis 12:1-3 with a promise given to Abraham. This promise was later formalised in chapters 15 and 17 into a covenant pact. In this formalisation of the promise, God pledges to provide Abraham's family their own land (15:8; 17:8). God also promises that Abraham will be the father of a great nation (17:4). This promise is not limited to Abraham, but will be an ongoing commitment to his descendants (17:7). God is the initiator of this covenant with Abraham. However, like the vassal-suzerain treaties, this covenant had conditions. Some of the vassal-suzerain treaties of the ancient Near East describe the two covenant parties walking between two rows of freshly killed animal flesh. This represented their fate (being torn in two) if they were disobedient or disloyal to the treaty. However in this account of Genesis 15, there is only one party that performs this ritual. In this ceremony to confirm or ratify the covenant only one party completes this pledge – God. This is significant as it is the suzerain (God) who places himself under the obligations of fulfilment and not the vassal, Abraham. It is God who leaves himself open to dismemberment should he violate the covenant agreement.[9]

Yet Abraham and his descendants also have a role to play. They must also "keep" the covenant (17:10-14). The sign of the covenant promise is that every male should be circumcised. This requirement allows for each new generation of Abraham's household to become part of the covenant people.[10] Those who are not circumcised will be cut off from the people of God. It was the identity marker of those who were to share in God's promises. So while it was a promise, they still had to participate in that grace by being faithful in circumcising their male children. This act represented their hope for their future children. They were cutting a part of the male body through which God's promise would be fulfilled. It showed that their hope was in God. In this sense it may also have been a sign of what would happen if the covenant was violated. God would no longer protect, and even cut off their future generations. However, this commitment to the blessing of Abraham and his descendants is pledged by God. It is also explicitly pledged to Isaac, the child of promise given to Abraham and his barren wife Sarah. Although Ishmael (the son from Abraham's liaison with Hagar) is blessed, he is deliberately excluded from the covenant (17:20). So it is through the lineage of Isaac and then Jacob that the nation of ancient Israel would form.

The book of Genesis establishes Abraham as the forefather of the people of ancient Israel in covenant with God. The covenant relationship of Abraham is continued by his "seed"; that is, by his family and subsequently the nation of ancient Israel. This promise becomes programmatic for the events and concerns of the rest of the Old Testament. Really, it sets the agenda for the rest of the bible.[11] God continues to protect and guide this covenant family. He blesses Isaac and his barren wife Rebekah with twin sons, Esau and Jacob. Of these boys, it is Jacob who is isolated as the son of promise. It is Jacob who will inherent the promise of Abraham. He, in turn, becomes the father of twelve sons. Jacob's name is changed to 'Israel' and his twelve sons would become the forefathers of the twelve tribes of Israel. This is the origin of their tribal structure. Each member of ancient Israel would be born into one of these tribes. It formed their identity.

As a nation, the covenant promises were not negated. They were to be God's special possession (his vassal) amongst all the peoples. But remember, their special status was not an end in itself. The purpose of their selection was to be a means of redemption for all humanity and creation. From Genesis onwards, the biblical narrative traces the story of the fulfilment of God's covenant promises with ancient Israel. They were liberated from Egypt and given specific laws to follow as part of their covenant relationship. They were established as a nation in their own land. Even though they failed to fulfil their covenant obligations, God showed continual grace to them through warnings spoken by the prophets. The prophets warned them of their eventual punishment because they rejected their covenant relationship. If they were a faithful vassal, they would be blessed. If they were an unfaithful vassal, they would be punished. Eventually, according to the covenant stipulations, the people were exiled. However, the prophets also reminded the people that the exile would not be the end. The ancient covenant promises would still be fulfilled as God would establish a new covenant with his people. That promise came to fruition in Jesus Christ.

Jesus, before going to the cross, shared a last meal with his disciples. At this meal he introduced a ritual which we know as the Lord's Supper, or communion. In Matt 26:26-30, the meal is represented as a covenant meal. Jesus sealed with his disciples a covenant that reminds us of God's covenant dealings in the Old Testament. The "new" covenant of Christ has its foundations in this Old Testament covenant of Abraham. Christ doesn't throw away or ignore the old covenants, but fulfils them. Jesus fulfils the covenant made with Abraham including its promises of descendants, land and blessings for the nations. However, as we noted in chapter 6, this fulfilment is not through a literal nation or land, but a community of faith. This faith is the same type demonstrated by Abraham. When we join this community of faith, we join the heritage of Abraham.

GROUP QUESTIONS:

1. From the account in Genesis 1, draw a table or diagram that demonstrates the pattern of creation. Discuss in your group the difference between humanity and animals.

2. How would you describe covenant to a non-Christian friend?

3. What questions would you ask of Abraham?

4. Read Genesis 39 (the story of Joseph and Potiphar's wife).

Apply the 'tools of the trade' to this passage:

i. What is the significance to *them*?
ii. What is the significance to *us*?
iii. What is the significance to *me*?

RECOMMENDED READING

⊰ Hayford, J., *Pursuing the Will of God: Reflections and Meditations on the Life of Abraham*, (Multnomah, 1997)

This is more of a devotional reflection on the life of Abraham than an academic work. Written by well-known Pentecostal pastor Jack Hayford, it will encourage and inspire you.

⊰ Bilezikian, Gilbert, *Community 101: Reclaiming the Local Church as a Community of Oneness*, (Zondervan, 1997).

This book presents a study of the theme of community. It establishes as its basis a reading of the creation accounts. From this philosophical foundation it then discusses ministry and leadership in the church. A very insightful read.

⊰ Clines, D.J.A., *The Theme of the Pentateuch*, 2nd ed., (Sheffield: SAP, 1997)

This is a more scholarly work, but is still accessible to most readers. It is based on a study of the patriarchal promises and how they provide the agenda for the rest of the Pentateuch.

ENDNOTES

1. In case you couldn't remember where this line comes from, it is the musical, *The Sound of Music.*

2. Charpentier, E., *How to Read the Bible: The Old and New Testaments,* (New York: Gramercy Books, 1981), p.19.

3. Grenz, Stanley, *Theology for the Community of God*, (Carlisle: Paternoster Press, 1994), pp.487-488.

4. Wilfong, Marsha, 'Human Creation in Canonical Context: Genesis 1:26-31 and Beyond' in Brown, W.P. & McBride, S.D. Jnr., (eds) *God Who Creates*, (Eerdmans, 2000), p.42.

5. The use of the word "helper" is often misconstrued as automatically implying that the one doing the helping is subservient to the one receiving the help. Some say that because Eve was Adam's helpmeet, she was positioned by God in a servant-like role, basically to assist him with his family and home. However the phrase used to describe the woman is *'ezer kenegdô*. Throughout the Old Testament, the word *'ezer* ('helper') is never used of a subordinate. Of the other 20 references to this word, 17 are references to God our helper, and the other 3 refer to a military ally (some of the references include Ex 18:4; Deut 33:7, 26, 29; Ps 20:2; 33:20; 70:5; 115:9, 10, 11; 121:1,2; 124:8; 146:5; Hosea 13:9; Is 30:5; Ezekiel 12:14; Daniel 11:34). However, she is not just a "helper" but an *'ezer kenegdô*. The term *kenegdô* means "corresponding to, equal to or matching". This word in Hebrew suggests an equal. She is neither superior nor inferior but equal. Eve was not given to serve Adam, but to serve with him, and to share the same tasks. So she is not identical but is an equal who complements as a perfectly fitted partner.

6. Longman, T., *Making Sense of the Old Testament: Three Crucial Questions*, (Grand Rapids, Michigan: Baker, 1998), p.62.

7. Longman, T., *Making Sense of the Old Testament: Three Crucial Questions*, p.62.

8. Longman, T., *Making Sense of the Old Testament: Three Crucial Questions*, p.65.

9. Hamilton, V.P., *The Book of Genesis Chapters 1-17*, NICOT, (Eerdmans, 1990), p.438.

10. Birch, B.C., Brueggemann, W., Fretheim, T.E., & Petersen, D.L., *A Theological Introduction to the Old Testament*, 2nd Ed., (Nashville: Abingdon, 2005), p.73.

11. This is the central thesis of Clines, D.J.A., *The Theme of the Pentateuch*, (Sheffield: SAP), 2nd edn, 1997.

Chapter 9

EXODUS AND THE LAW

Throughout the testimony of ancient Israel so far, we have seen how God is revealed. God is revealed as the awesome creator, the concerned parent, covenant partner and suzerain king. Each event in the testimony of ancient Israel so far demonstrates the need of humanity for a saviour. Yet, it also demonstrates God's faithfulness in blessing the covenant people. By the beginning of the book of Exodus, God's promise to Abraham of descendants "more numerous than the stars in the sky" (Gen 15:4-5) is fulfilled. The book of Exodus begins by noting how the Israelites had multiplied greatly, so that the land was filled with them (Ex 1:7). God was faithful to his promise to Abraham. God was faithful to the creation blessing given to humanity in Genesis 1. However, the book of Exodus tells us that the Israelites increased in such numbers that the Egyptians began to fear for their own security (Ex 1:8-22).

Because of this threat to Egypt, the descendants of Abraham were persecuted and enslaved. Yet, they continued to increase because God was faithful to the covenant promise. Even when Pharaoh decreed for the death of their male babies, they prospered through the cunning initiative of their midwives. It was in this situation of desperation and intrigue that Moses was born. The biblical testimony tells us that Moses was raised in the household of Pharaoh. He would play a key role in the liberation of the ancient Israelites from their slavery. God would send Moses as a deliverer for the people. God did this out of commitment to the covenant promise. Exodus 2:23 tells us how the people groaned in their slavery. God heard them and acted because of his covenant with Abraham and his descendants.

God acted to liberate them because of his promise to Abraham. God continues to act out of commitment to the promises made to his covenant people. The term 'exodus' means to literally "go out" - and that's what they did. Through the direction of God, they left behind their place of slavery in Egypt. But it wasn't smooth sailing. There was a battle for the possession of these people. Would they belong to Pharaoh or to God?

God acted at the exodus to fulfil his part of the covenant. However God also acted to help the people fulfil their part. Whenever they were under the control of Pharaoh, they could not be faithful to their covenant relationship with God. Pharaoh was considered divine by the ancient Egyptians. As we noted in chapter 4, the Egyptian religion considered their land to be stewarded by Amon-Re's son, the Pharaoh, who was made in his image. Pharaoh was considered divine. Therefore while the ancient Israelites were subservient to this Pharaoh, their loyalty was divided. They were serving both Pharaoh and God. They were unable to be loyal worship or be in exclusive relationship with their covenant God. They needed a saviour. What was the reason Moses gave Pharaoh for the people leaving? He says: "Let my people go, that they may serve me" (7:16, 8:1). God required their exclusive loyalty. God commissioned Moses to bring "my people" forth in order to "serve" God upon the mountain (3:10). The future of ancient Israel was not in service of Pharaoh, but in service of God. It is at this point that ancient Israel becomes identified by an important term: God's Son. Moses says to Pharaoh in Exodus 4:22 "Thus says the Lord, Israel is my firstborn son, and I say to you, 'Let my son go that he may serve me." (TNIV). So God provided them liberation and freedom. But this freedom required their faith and trust.

However, there was a problem - as there so often is! The arrogance of Pharaoh would not allow his slaves to be released.[1] What follows is a show-down between God and Pharaoh. Who is the more powerful God? Is it the gods of Egypt or Yahweh, the

God of creation?[2] Through a series of ten great and terrible plagues, God wages war against Pharaoh. These plagues are progressively destructive until God is proved the most powerful. All of creation obeys his commands. God defeats Pharaoh. The armies of Pharaoh are conquered at the Reed Sea – the very place in their mythology that Amon-Re was supposed to rise victorious. Instead, it is the place of Pharaoh's defeat. The community of ancient Israel were able to cross through the waters of the Reed Sea like a cleansing baptism away from their former life. The exodus revealed to the ancient Israelites that Yahweh was a god of power. Yahweh was and is *the* God. The Song of Moses in Exodus 15 celebrates God as a warrior. God liberated them with a "mighty hand". Once again, God functions like a suzerain – a great king – who defends, protects and graciously liberates his covenant people.

Many students are concerned with the historical veracity of the exodus event. This is a difficult question, because it is extremely difficult to date the exodus event. The biblical testimony is concerned with theological meaning of the events rather than history in the modern sense of the word. Their testimony doesn't even bother to give the specific name of the Pharaoh.[3] They were interested in inspiring faith and obedience to God. Although the biblical account provides no historical report in the modern sense of the term, there are some indications of the setting. Opinions differ as to when the exodus would have occurred, however most authorities place the exodus in the 13th century BCE.[4] Yet ultimately, despite the variety of archaeological evidence, the biblical witness is clear that God delivered his covenant people.

The exodus is the central event of the Old Testament. It was continually referred to as the evidence of God's love and power. It would be celebrated and remembered in the yearly festivals, such as the Passover. God had delivered his people with an awesome demonstration of power. The exodus would become a reminder of the trustworthiness and faithfulness of God. In new situations of challenge and threat, the people remembered the exodus. They remembered God's deliverance. If God did it once, he could do it again. Psalm 136 draws on this testimony to encourage them that when confronted with overwhelming odds or a task that seemed impossible, they were to remember the exodus and trust in the power of God to deliver them. The exodus gives hope for the future. The prophets of ancient Israel also continually referred to the exodus event to remind the people of God's power to deliver. Isaiah 40:1-11, 28-31 uses the imagery of the exodus to speak to the people confronted with the catastrophe of the exile. God would provide for them in the desert. He would carry them as on eagle's wings. The prophet used the images to give faith and hope to the people. Just as God delivered them once, God could do it again. If God could deliver them from Egypt, then God could lead a second exodus out of exile.

The exodus is also a concept used in the New Testament. The story of the exodus of ancient Israel from bondage to freedom is used to represent the meaning of redemption and salvation. The concept of being delivered from slavery into freedom is the basis for our definition of atonement. We use this event of the exodus to describe the work of Jesus at the cross. While this redemption was achieved physically in the exodus event as ancient Israel was liberated from physical bondage into physical freedom, deliverance in the New Testament is through the atonement of Christ. Jesus has redeemed us from the slavery of sin and liberated us with a "mighty hand". Our understanding of the cross is founded on this event and the meaning of freedom that it carries. The exodus of the Old Testament speaks of our salvation in Christ. Yet, while it speaks of our final corporate destiny as Christians, it can also represent our personal journey. Each of us has challenges in our journey of discipleship. For each of us, the concept of "Egypt" can represent different types of slavery. It can represent a former lifestyle, habits or practices that have held us in some kind of bondage. While we may have become Christians, we are still held back by this bondage of slavery through our habits of thinking or behaviour. Perhaps we have stayed in the slavery of addiction, or low self-esteem. Christ calls us to leave this place of slavery. We are called to leave behind our former habits and actions that conflict with the nature of our faith in Jesus Christ. Our challenge is this: what do we need to leave behind in our personal "Egypt"?

For ancient Israel, they had a lot to leave behind in Egypt. This was harder than we may think. Although Egypt was the place of slavery, there was a level of comfort and security in that bondage. They had to leave their old identity as slaves. They had to leave behind their trust in themselves and their own provision from the predictable produce of Egypt. They had to leave this for a new identity and a new life of faith. Their new life of faith required them to trust in God their deliverer to provide their daily needs. God proved faithful through the miraculous daily provision of manna-bread and meat. The exodus also provided them with a new identity. This new identity was given to them at the mountain of Sinai in Exodus 19: 1- 6. This description given of God's liberation of the people of ancient Israel is like a mother bird carrying her young to safety (Ex 19:4). It describes them as being carried like on eagles wings at the exodus. It was here that they would re-form their covenant with God. The people had left Egypt to travel through the wilderness to the mountain of worship. Yet, although the people were travelling to the Promised Land, they did not go there directly. The people had to get Egypt out of their thinking before they could live in the new land.[5]

At Sinai they re-forged their covenant relationship. However it would not be as a family group but as a nation. God had delivered them and adopted them to be his special covenant people. They were his "son". This event was restoring them to their original function given at creation to reflect the image of God. They were now God's people. They had a special identity as God's treasured possession. This was not because they were necessarily more special in themselves, but because God had graciously chosen them (Deut 7:6-8). They were one group of people delivered in a common, redemptive act. Just like us in Christ, they were also called to share a common identity, lifestyle and common destiny. There are two phrases used to describe this new identity in Exodus 19 that we will examine a little more closely.

The testimony of ancient Israel records the speech of God to them in Exodus 19. They were called to be a "kingdom or priests" and a "holy nation". What does this mean? The concept of priesthood was familiar to all the nations in the ancient Near East world. Priests were particular people who were given specific roles and responsibilities in the worship of a god. They were representatives of a god to people, and represented the people to a god. They functioned as mediators. Yet, for ancient Israel it wasn't just any god that they were called to serve but the liberating God, creator of the world. Ancient Israel was called as an entire nation to be a kingdom of priests. They were to be representatives of God to the nations of the world, and represent the nations of the world to God. As priests, their vocation was worship. This was their new identity.

Further, ancient Israel was also called to be a "holy nation". This meant they were set apart for the purposes and glory of God. The Old Testament continually affirms holiness as an essential characteristic of God. Holiness is a difficult concept to define. It does not mean that God is removed and distant. Neither does it equate God with moral purity – although it can include these ideas. Holiness suggests an innate beauty. As God was holy, so the people were called to reflect this essential characteristic. As vassals they were to reflect the nature and character of their suzerain. They were to reflect God's holiness. Similarly, for *us* as Christian readers, we have been given a new identity in Christ. As ancient Israel was identified as the people of God in the exodus, so we also are identified as the people of God through Christ. The New Testament adopts this language of the exodus to describe for the Christian believers their new vocation. According to 1 Peter 2:9, we are to be a holy nation and royal priesthood. This does not look the same as it did for ancient Israel, as we are not a political entity. We are people bonded by faith living in all the nations of the world, not a single citizenship. Our vocation is to reflect the nature and character of our liberator and suzerain, Jesus Christ.

How is this passage significant to *them, us & me*? The significance might be demonstrated by the following illustration. Once again, it is my personal attempt to symbolically represent the message of Exodus 19:1-6. It represents the significance of this verse for *them, us & me*.

The significance to *them* is:

- God has liberated them from Egypt by carrying them on eagles wings (*represented by the bird*)

- They have left the place of bondage (*see the bars signifying a gaol*)

- They have been led to Sinai where they will reform their covenant (the centre mountain). This place also represents their new identity of being set apart as a "holy nation" (*the centre mountain is set apart and 'morally' higher than the other mountains*). Yet, they are to function in the word as God's representatives (*the centre mountain is surrounded by other mountains signifying the other nations*)

The significance to *us* is:

- Jesus Christ has delivered us from the bondage of our sin (*represented by the bird*)

- We also have a new identity in Christ as God's special people, set apart and holy (*represented by the centre mountain*)

- Yet, while we are not of this world, we live in the world and demonstrate the character of God to people that do not yet know him (*the centre mountain is surrounded by other mountains signifying the nations*)

Although this will be different for each reader, **the significance to me** is:

- There are specific bondages of Egypt that I need to leave behind (*see the bars signifying a gaol*) so I can soar, like on eagles wings, with Christ

While this relationship between God and ancient Israel was established at Sinai, what would it actually look like? How would this covenant relationship impact their daily lives and social interactions? This relationship between God and ancient Israel was further defined by the legal, formal expression of their relationship in their covenant agreement. This was the law. It gave definition and parameters to their relationship with God. God was their suzerain.

He was their protector and provider. Ancient Israel was to be God's servants. They were required to obey God. They were not to obey the law for the sake of the law, but to obey God (who had given them these guidelines).[6] Yet, the law gave the boundaries and expectation of how the vassal should respond to the suzerain. It is essential to remember that God was their redeemer before their lawgiver. This law outlined their expected behaviour and their new code of conduct. It provided structure.

Structure is crucial for an ordered society. Just as God ordered and structured creation in Genesis 1, God now gives ancient Israel structure and rules to live by.[7] In this sense, the law was a gracious gift from God. It provided a source of meditation and delight for the righteous person (Psalm 1). It provided the guidance of God for their nation. The law provided the picture of how they were to live as God's representatives in their culture and time. They were no longer slaves. They must now live as dignified and responsible people within their new nation. With God as their king, they must establish structure and rules for their self-governance. The law provided them with these principles for living that reflects God's guidance. However, the law was not just a good idea. It was there to be obeyed. There were consequences as to whether the law was obeyed or disobeyed. The ancient Israelites would be blessed if they obeyed, but cursed if they disobeyed (Deut 28). Yet this covenant relationship not only governed how they treated each other, but also regulated their worship of God. Their worship was formalised by the introduction of the temple and sacrificial system. The definition and boundaries of their worship was endorsed by God.

The law acted as the regulator of their relationship with God and each other. It gave concrete shape to how the vassal should live in grateful response to their suzerain.[8] These requirements of ancient Israel are contained mainly in four of the five books of the Pentateuch (in the books of Exodus, Leviticus, Numbers and re-iterated in Deuteronomy). The laws deal with all kinds of issues, including the relationship between God and humanity as well as the relationship between human beings. It is common among contemporary scholars to distinguish three types of Old Testament laws: moral law, civil and ceremonial law.[9] The moral law presents God's principles for living. They are the values (or morals) out of which the specific laws are drawn. The most well-known example of moral law is the "Ten Commandments" (Ex 20). They provide the philosophical and ethical foundation in how people should live. At the centre of this revelation, is the liberating, creator God (Ex 20:1). This is how they were to reflect their status as God's chosen people. This moral law is summed up by Jesus in Luke 10:27 in the statement: "You must love the Lord your God with all your heart, all your soul, all your strength and all your mind. And, 'love your neighbour as yourself'" (TNIV).

In comparison, the civic law is the application of the moral law. These are the laws that regulated how ancient Israel as a single community was to live in their daily interaction. It interprets the moral law specific to its culture and time. It is usually presented as 'case laws' – specific scenarios in which the moral law is applied. As we read the case laws, we see that all the laws of the Old Testament flow from the ethical principles established in the Ten Commandments. They are not additions, but flow from the principles.[10] It also includes the laws that regulated ancient Israel's governance. As we read these civil laws, they seem a world away from our contemporary situation. And guess what? They are! We live in a completely different type of world to this pre-industrial, illiterate society. What, then should we do with a case law like Exodus 21: 28-30 about a bull that gores someone to death? It does not seem very relevant to most of us in an urban society. Tremper Longman gives an insightful analysis. The purpose of the case law regarding the goring ox is to protect life.[11] If an ox gores a person to death it must be destroyed, but the owner who didn't know any better at the time is not responsible. However if the ox has done this before and the owner does nothing and it kills a second person, then the owner is responsible and must be punished.

The owner, through negligence or rejection of the law has caused the death of another person. Therefore they are guilty of murder, breaking the sixth commandment. So the case law is an outworking of the ethical principle: do not murder.

What Longman notes is it that the general ethical principles of the Ten Commandments are still current for New Testament believers. They are still the moral ideals which we live by. Clearly Jesus and the apostles appealed to the many principles of the Ten Commandments. They identified violations of these principles, such as idolatry, blasphemy, cursing one's parents, stealing, murder and adultery, as wrong. However, exactly how we specifically live out these principles has changed. The application of the Ten Commandments has changed for Christians today. We are no longer necessarily agriculturalists, and we are no longer a distinct nation. Our identity as the people of God is no longer based on ethnicity or living in a social-geographic location. We are the people of God scattered throughout the nations of the world. We are living in a different point in redemptive history. Yet we can see principles of living that please God in the Ten Commandments that we also need to apply. But we adapt the application of the moral principle to our specific situation. In the case of the goring ox, we see the principle that God values life. I might not have a bull, but I might have a bulldog. I am responsible to make sure that my bulldog does not endanger the life of anyone. By doing this, in whatever country and law-code, I am fulfilling the moral law of God.

But as we can see from the testimony of ancient Israel as well as our own experience, it is impossible for humanity to hold perfectly to the law. As Paul says in Rom 3:20, the more we know the law, the clearer it becomes that we are not obeying it! We know that we are law-breakers because not only do our actions contradict the law, but also our motivations. So Christ came to complete that role for us. He came to fulfil the law (Matt 5:17). So we now interpret the law through Christ. Christ tells us that it is not only our actions but our motivations that are important for Christian living. We are not only to love one another in actions, but in motivation as well. And we are given the Spirit to help us in this daily walk (Gal 5:14, 15).

As part of the covenant relationship with ancient Israel, God not only provided the moral and civil law but also established official forms and means of worship. This is often referred to as the ceremonial law. Worship was central to the experience of ancient Israel in relating to God. It was the response of the ancient Israelites in their covenant dealings with God. Their worship was meant to reflect the nature and character of the God they served. The term for the form or the expression of worship in concrete acts performed in a community is called 'cult'. It comes from the French language to refer to the rituals and actions used in worship (and is not a reference to any occult practices!). Their worship took a definite form. The covenant provided the rules regulating the priesthood, worship, sacrificial rituals and the place of worship. These concepts and institutions were widespread in the ancient Near Eastern world. So when God instituted these systems, it was a form that the people were already familiar with.[12] God used their culture to bring new meaning and purpose in their worship.

The covenant established a special place for their worship, the tabernacle. This was a portable sanctuary where God would symbolically dwell. At the centre was the 'Holy Place'. It contained the 'ark of the covenant' that symbolised and was God's presence amongst them. The ark was mobile, so it was carried by the priests in their journeys. Whenever they moved location or changed camp in the desert, it was this 'ark of the covenant' that led them through the wilderness. It also led the nation in warfare. They were led by God as king (Numbers 10:33-36). As other nations would march into battle led by their human king, so ancient Israel would march behind the ark that symbolised God as their king, leading them into battle. The tabernacle, containing the ark was placed in the centre of the camp when the people are at rest. The tabernacle became Israel's portable worship centre, and symbolised that God had come to live among his covenant people. Here Israel could worship and fellowship with God. It was later replaced by the permanent structure of the Temple. But for about 450 years the tabernacle would be the central place for ancient Israel's worship.

In this place of worship, they would perform specific forms of worship. However, you couldn't just go into the tabernacle at any time, but had to meet with God in a special process of worship called the sacrifices. This is also sometimes called the Levitical system. These ceremonial laws and instructions are mostly recorded in the books of Exodus and Leviticus. This system was used for the people to right their relationship with God and each other. The animal sacrifices they offered had some form of sanctifying function. They were also very costly within an agricultural society. When the people sinned, they needed to find cleansing to be readmitted into the presence of God and restore their relationship with God. The blood provided this. As mentioned already, God would set apart certain people, known as priests, to attend to the matters of the place and worship.[13] While ancient Israel was to be a kingdom of priests, there was later appointed a specific tribe (the Levites) to administer the offering system. This religious system and rituals of the Old Testament were never intended to be just an outward form. They were meant to reflect the inward worship of their heart. Yet the outward expression of worship did have an important place in ancient Israelite worship. Although the symbolic significance of the cult was quite different to how we often view worship.

Relationship with God for the ancient Israelites was not just about direct personal communion, but was also expressed through physical representation and bodily actions. These actions and representations included kneeling and prostration in prayer, dancing, marking off sacred enclosures from the common ground, separating people as priests and the preparation of sacrifices and solemn sacrifices. All these visible things were soaked with symbolic meaning. In particular, it emphasised the characteristics of God whom they worshiped. Not only the lifestyle but also the worship of ancient Israel was required to reflect the holiness of God. They were a holy people. They were to live as holy people. Should the people sin (taint that holiness), then the worship system provided a way for them to be cleansed and get right again. It reminded them they could not get right on their own, but needed a saviour. As Christian readers, we are also required to reflect the holiness and character of our saviour (1 Peter 1:13-16).

The New Testament tells us that in our saviour Jesus Christ, the Word became flesh and tabernacled among us. In John 1:14, the body of Jesus is described as a tabernacle-tent. Within this tent was the glory of the Lord, just like ancient Israel's tabernacle. John continues to say that "we have seen his glory". When Jesus cleansed the Temple (John 2:13-33) he said, "Destroy this Temple, and I will raise it up in three days". After his resurrection the disciples figured out he was talking about his body. His body was the true temple in which the glory resided. And when the physical body of Jesus was destroyed, so was the system used in the actual temple in Jerusalem. The curtain in the Holy Place was torn in two. The cross ended the Levitical system of worship. Through the Spirit, the believer has become the temple of God (1 Cor.3:16-17; 6:19). This was the new covenant promised by Jeremiah that a new covenant would be made not on stone but on the hearts of believers. Together, believers comprise the "body of Christ". Together we form the Temple of the Holy Spirit (1 Peter 2:4-5). Consequently for the Christian church, there is no central holy place where believers must attend and enter with the ritual of sacrifices. Instead, this ritual has been completed once for all by Christ – the only "Temple" we enter to be purified and sanctified.

Yet it is important that as we read about the laws and worship of ancient Israel that we don't belittle its value. The law was God's provision and grace for that time. It was loved and cherished by the people (as noted in Psalm 1). It was part of the covenant relationship of ancient Israel. The same God who miraculously delivered them from Egypt was the same God who provided the structures for their new life. However it would be another forty years before the people would enter this place of rest. This first generation of ex-slaves rejected the guidance of God. They did not respond in faith to the journey. Instead, it would be their children, the second generation, who would enter the land of promise. This narrative of the wilderness wanderings is presented in the book of Numbers. As a result of their hesitancy, this group of ex-slaves were led by Moses from Sinai to the plains of Moab. At Moab, Moses re-affirmed the law. The book of Deuteronomy outlines this final speech of Moses. It gave directions in how they were to live in the land. It outlined for them how to care, manage and maintain the land as responsible land-owners. They were no longer slaves. The privilege of leading the people into the land would not be given to Moses, but to Joshua. It is to the testimony of Joshua that we turn next.

GROUP DISCUSSION QUESTIONS:

1. Describe what happened at the exodus?

2. What was the main idea of the covenant at Mt Sinai (Exodus 19-20)?

3. How is worship in your church similar to the worship system in the Old Testament.

4. Read Exodus 32:1-33:6 (story of the golden calf). Apply the 'tools of the trade' to this passage:

    i.   What is the significance to *them*?
    ii. What is the significance to *us*?
    iii. What is the significance to *me*?

RECOMMENDED READING

ఇ₊ Fretheim, Terrence E., *The Pentateuch*, IBT, (Abingdon, 1996)

This gives a solid and informative overview of the five books of the Pentateuch. It does engage scholarly issues, but also discusses some juicy topics such as the providence of God.

ఇ₊ Ross, Allen P., *Holiness to the Lord*, (Baker, 2002)

This is an excellent commentary on the book of Leviticus. It is quite easy to read and gives great insight into this often neglected book.

ENDNOTES:

1. The hardening of Pharaoh's heart in the Book of Exodus is a much debated concept. When God first calls and sends Moses to confront Pharaoh, there is a recognition that Pharaoh is both arrogant and proud. This pride and tendency toward obstinacy is described as his 'hardness of heart'. The debate mainly focuses on whether this is a description or prescription (ie is God making / pre-destining his heart to be hard or is it a description of what his tendency is and expected outcome). This latter approach suggests that his pride and arrogance is a prior reality - God/Moses' actions merely intensify it. His pattern of will-ful arrogance then becomes irreversible. So Pharaoh is expected to be pride-ful (!) and unrelenting, which is exactly how he responds (remember its a re-telling, so a narrative recorded much later after the events it is describing). For further discussion on this see Fretheim, T.E., *The Pentateuch*, IBT, (Nashville: Abingdon, 1996).

2. Birch, B.C., Brueggemann, W., Fretheim, T.E., & Petersen, D.L., *A Theological Introduction to the Old Testament*, 2nd Ed., (Nashville: Abingdon, 2005), pp.100-101.

3. Birch, B.C., Brueggemann, W., Fretheim, T.E., & Petersen, D.L., *A Theological Introduction to the Old Testament*, 2nd Ed, p.98.

4. Fretheim, T.E., *The Pentateuch*, IBT, (Nashville: Abingdon, 1996), p.102.

5. Fretheim, T.E., *The Pentateuch*, p.110.

6. Birch, B.C., Brueggemann, W., Fretheim, T.E., & Petersen, D.L., *A Theological Introduction to the Old Testament*, p,162.

7. Birch, B.C., Brueggemann, W., Fretheim, T.E., & Petersen, D.L., *A Theological Introduction to the Old Testament*, p.127.

8. Longman, T., *Making Sense of the Old Testament: Three Crucial Questions*, p.65.

9. Longman, T., *Making Sense of the Old Testament: Three Crucial Questions*, p.110. Though Longman does note that the Israelites themselves did not separate them into these categories.

10. Longman, T., *Making Sense of the Old Testament: Three Crucial Questions*, p.116.

11. Longman, T., *Making Sense of the Old Testament: Three Crucial Questions*, pp 114-115.

12. Ross, A.P., *Holiness to the Lord*, (Baker, 2002), pp.21-28.

13. Ross, A.P., *Holiness to the Lord*, p. 73

Chapter 10

Taking and Living in the Land

Our study of the testimony of ancient Israel so far has emphasised God as creator. As described in Genesis 1, a special act of that creation was the formation of humanity by royal decree. Humanity was created to be in unique relationship with God. However, with this unique relationship came responsibility. Humanity was created to shine the character and knowledge of God to the rest of the world. They were also required to multiply and fill the earth as part of the blessing of the Creator. The attempt of humanity to fulfil these roles, beginning with the first couple, was quite disastrous. But God did not give up. He then focused on one family that would become the vehicle of redemption. This family would be in special, covenant relationship with God. Through many trials, they survived. The ultimate trial was in Egypt. They were enforced into slavery. But God did not forget them. God did not forget his covenant promise. He rescued them. In probably the most miraculous and world-changing event in the Old Testament, the ancient Israelites were redeemed from Egypt. They became God's "son". So far in the testimony of ancient Israel we have seen God revealed as creator, parent, suzerain and redeemer. Now we will see God revealed to the people as warrior and king.

At the exodus, the family group of Abraham became a nation in covenant relationship with God. They were slaves no more. Their next challenge was to live like a nation ruled by God. The law given during the exodus from Egypt gave them the boundaries to live in community under God's rule. It gave structure and order to their society. The law, as defined further by Deuteronomy, gave them specific instructions in how to live in the land of promise. They had the law, now all they needed was a place to live. The Pentateuch (the first five books) ends with ancient Israel perched on the edge of this land of promise. They are ready to take it. The new generation led by Joshua would be a people of faith. This land would be the fulfilment of the promises to Abraham, Isaac and Jacob. It was a gift from God (Deut 6:10-11; Deut 8:7-10).[1] The same God who provided directly for them in the wilderness with manna, meat and water from the rock, now provides them with houses, vineyards and crops and cisterns already built – the instruments of production and the ability to feed themselves.[2]

The theme of land is extremely important in the Old Testament. To study this theme, we will look primarily at the next section of the Old Testament – the Former Prophets (or historical books). These books deal mainly with the testimony of how ancient Israel were established and lived in the land. The land was the place where they were to live under God's law, guidance and blessing. They were required to care for the land as good stewards under the direction of their creator.[3] In this land they were destined to live as a people of faith with God as their king. Their new home would be God's kingdom where God's rule was established. Their king (God) would lead them into battle to take the land by military force. God would be their military leader. Although in saying this, the land would not be taken by the superior weaponry or military skill of ancient Israel. Instead, they were totally reliant on God. This theme of the divine warrior is closely connected with the concept of covenant. This is emphasised by their first action of ancient Israel once they had crossed the Jordan.

The first action of the people in the land was to circumcise the new generation. This second generation of ex-slaves were the continuation of the people of God. The new generation had to participate in the sign of the covenant. This would not have been a smart military strategy in the natural. It would have made them vulnerable. But through it they demonstrated their reliance on God. It was obviously more dangerous for them to go into battle spiritually unprepared (that is, uncircumcised) rather than physically disadvantaged.[4] In this action, they recognised that they would achieve the land by God's workings. Yet, they still had to participate in this fight. The land would not be handed to them on a platter. They had to fight. But they must fight as people of faith, reliant on God. The only requirement was faith and obedience. Once the people had crossed the Jordan, entered the land and renewed the covenant through circumcision, their leader Joshua confronted an unusual person. In Joshua 5:13-15, on the eve of their first battle at Jericho, the leader encountered an unknown figure with a drawn sword. This figure was God revealed in the guise of a warrior.

In the book of Joshua we see one of the most dramatic revelations of this aspect of the character of God in the Old Testament. The soldier identified himself as the "commander of the army of the Lord" (Josh 5:13-15). However Joshua's response, like that of Moses at the burning bush, leaves us in no doubt that this is God himself. A remarkable strategy is given which results in the destruction of the walls of Jericho without the Israelites even touching them. They are to march around the city led by the 'ark of the covenant'. This 'ark of the covenant' was the symbol and presence of God amongst them. It was God as king leading the people. This action of circling the city was a bold military statement that claimed the territory as part of the rule of God. God as their king was taking the land of promise. The taking of Jericho is described in the testimony of ancient Israel as a miraculous event. It demonstrated that God fights for and wins the battle on behalf of his covenant people of faith. It demonstrated that God was active in the unseen spiritual world. This unseen spiritual world directed the events in the natural. It reminds us that there is more to this world than meets the eye.[5] For ancient Israel, there were different forces in this unseen spiritual realm that were at war with one another. This worldview continues in the New Testament as well (see for example, Ephesians 6:10-20).

This story from Joshua 5 also highlights some important principles of battle preparation. Warfare was not just a military function, but theologically significant. Physical war was a spiritual battle in which the gods battled with one another. God wages war against these forces that are seeking to destroy his good plan for creation. Although it is a spiritual battle, God works through his covenant people. At Jericho, it is God's presence (represented by the 'ark of the covenant') that causes the walls to crumble and the people to win victory. Yet, the human actors had a role in this battle as the Joshua passage reminds us. God promised to protect ancient Israel against their enemies as long as they remained faithful and loyal to him (Deut 28:7). In other words, God would be a divine warrior who would protect them.[6] God wins the victories for ancient Israel. Although they may fight, it is not their own strength or superiority which brings success, but it is because God is with them.

The role of the people was always to be obedient to the guidance and law of God. When the people were disobedient, the worst possible sentence that the prophets could threaten was banishment from the land or exile. Consequently, the people would *keep* the land, not by their military strength or force, but by obedience to their covenant God.[7] So God promises to fight on behalf of his people as they are faithful to the covenant. He promises military and physical help when the people trust him. However, he also indicates that he will abandon them, even work against them, if they are disloyal (Deut 28:25-26). As the blessing of divine military victory flows from obedience to the covenant, so defeat will follow disobedience. These were not just idle threats in Deuteronomy, but carried out if they were not obedient. This is particularly demonstrated in Joshua 7 when the ancient Israelites failed to capture the city of Ai. This failure was not due to the military strength of the people of Ai, but because one of the ancient Israelites had disobeyed their instructions. Once this issue of disobedience was dealt with, they went on to capture the city. Their success in battle was determined by their faithfulness to the covenant relationship.

God had promised to protect his chosen people, but that didn't mean they could battle whomever they wanted in whatever way they chose. They had to discern God's will before they engaged in any military campaign.[8] This lesson would be demonstrated again and again throughout the testimony of the Old Testament. Ancient Israel had to be clear that God was directing them into battle. Joshua 5 demonstrates that God both commissioned and imparted war strategy to Joshua.[9] When the ancient Israelites captured Jericho, they burned the city including all the inhabitants (except Rahab and her family (6:17-25)). The word for this total destruction is *herem* (devotion or ban). This practice was the total annihilation of the people, livestock, and religious centres.[10] So it was not just the defeat of Jericho, but their destruction. This practice followed God's command (Deut.7:1-11; 20:16-18). Other options of defeat may have been to construct a treaty relationship with the vanquished nation and demand tribute or taxes to be regularly sent (Deut.12:29-31; 20:16-18). However, the people groups living inside the land of promise were to be *herem*, annihilated.

This aspect of the testimony of ancient Israel presents an ethical dilemma to many contemporary readers. The practice of herem seems contrary to the New Testament concept of a loving God, and is offensive to many. What is described as 'promised' and 'given' in reality is taken with brutal force by an army described as led by God and approved by God. Does God sanction mass homicide?[11] This claim to land entitlement is also part of the ongoing force behind the politics and territorial ambitions of the present state of Israel. However, Scripture's answer is that the Canaanites brought this destruction upon themselves by their own wickedness (Gen 15:16; Deut 9:4-5).[12] The religion practised in Canaan was particularly corrupt and disgusting. The people of Canaan considered their gods to have an extremely low moral character, so the morality of the people was extremely low.

The Canaanites in Joshua's day practiced child sacrifice, sacred prostitution, and snake worship. If allowed to remain, these practices would have corrupted ancient Israel – as indeed they later did. Therefore, ancient Israel was charged to destroy the Canaanites for two reasons. Firstly, it was to punish them for their abhorrent practices (Gen 15:16; 2). Secondly, it was to prevent contamination of ancient Israel (Deut 12:29-31; Deut 20:16-18; Lev 18). The destruction of the inhabitants is likened by LaSor, to the need to remove an arm or leg or even a vital organ when life is at stake.[13] Like such surgery, the annihilation of the Canaanites is considered by scholars to be a unique response to a exceptional situation. However, because ancient Israel did not completely eradicate the inhabitants from the land, they became contaminated by Canaanite practises and experienced the judgement of God themselves.

The continuation of the testimony of ancient Israel through the book of Judges describes their decline into the idolatry and practices of the Canaanites. It did not take long for the tribes of ancient Israel to be contaminated by the religion of their neighbours. They were influenced by the people groups they did not remove from the land (Judges 1:1-2:5). Ancient Israel had disobeyed God by not driving out all of the inhabitants. Therefore God would not drive them out for ancient Israel either (Judges 2:20-23). Because the Canaanites continued to control the plains, the Israelites settled on the more sparsely populated hills. Here the soil was poorer and there was less water for their crops. This led them to believe that Baal was more successful as a god who provided fertility and storms.[14] And so established in the land, ancient Israel turns to the worship of other gods (Judges 2:6-16). Their co-habitation proves a spiritual test. A testing which clearly demonstrated two truths. Firstly, it demonstrated that God is faithful to the covenant even though his people are not. Secondly, it demonstrated that when the people call upon God, he will deliver them.

We see in the book of Judges a cycle. It is a pattern that is observed throughout the testimony of ancient Israel. Actually, it is a pattern also observable in the lives of many Christian believers. This pattern begins with God's provision. This provision is followed by a turning or slipping away. Because the people have turned from God and his law, they then inflame the judgement of God. Through the harshness of this punishment the people repent. They cry out to God to deliver them. God is faithful. He hears their cry and fights on behalf of his people as the divine warrior. God responds with deliverance and provision. However, the people become either complacent or rebellious, so they turn away from this provision of God. Because the people have turned from God and his law, then they inflame the judgement of God. And so the cycle continues.

We see this same pattern repeated again and again in the book of Judges (see, for example, Judges 4-5). The people ignored their covenant relationship with God and turned to the worship of the Canaanite gods. God judged them by handing them over to other nations for punishment. The people cried out in their helplessness. So God raised a deliverer (usually called a 'judge') to rescue the people. This situation led to the rise of an important type of leadership known as 'charismatic leadership'. There were two main forms of leadership in ancient Israel. Firstly, there was the leadership of the judges ('charismatic leadership'). They represented God as king in delivering the people. However the people did not want to be ruled by an unseen God. They wanted an earthly king like all the other nations. So God relented. From there they developed a system of government based on kingship called 'monarchy'. This would be the main form of government practised in ancient Israel.

In the book of Judges, there was no king. God was the king (this is called a theocracy). Instead, the judges were raised up by God in this period of disorganisation to lead his people. There was no centralised structure of leadership, but the people were governed on a tribal basis. The 'charismatic leaders' or judges were military leaders during times of deliverance (2:16; 3:9,15). Warfare at this time tended to be tribally based. The military forces were recruited from the tribe and motivated by the protection of the local tribe.[15] However, during peace time, the 'charismatic leaders' functioned as legal or judicial figures (4:4-5). These leaders were not only raised up by God, but they were also equipped by the Spirit of God to perform their ministry (3:10; 6:34; 11:29).

The Holy Spirit in the Old Testament was not necessarily given to all people in the community. The Spirit would come upon an individual for a purpose. They were chosen by God and acted on behalf of God to lead and deliver the people. The Spirit would also equip individuals for the role of prophet and king. However this was not the experience of the whole community. The Spirit (at this time) would only come upon chosen individuals. Their only qualification was that God had chosen them. This assured the leaders of divine inspiration and direct guidance from God. This also meant that the leadership of the judges was not permanent. It wasn't passed on to their children like a dynasty but ended with either the death of the leader or the fulfilment of the purpose. This meant that there was little stability in their ongoing government. There was a lack of consistent administrative order. It also meant that the tribes were under continual threat from outside attack. The period is well summed up in Judges 21:25: "In those days Israel had no king: everyone did as they saw fit" (TNIV).

This type of temporal and informal leadership is hard to sustain. The next type of leadership introduced in the Old Testament addresses this by providing administrative order and longevity. It was the introduction of kingship, or a monarchy (1 Sam 8:1-9). In terms of the ancient Near East, the monarchy in ancient Israel is seen as quite a late development. Scholars generally give two reasons for the development of kingship in ancient Israel. The first was the increasing threat of the Philistines. The Philistines were another group living in the Palestine region (more along the coast) that began to expand their territory. Because of this threat, ancient Israel needed a stronger, more centralised form of government. The Philistines were militarily and politically stronger than ancient Israel. For example, they controlled the production of iron. This meant that all ancient Israelites had to go to a Philistine to have their farming instruments sharpened (1 Sam 13:16-22). The second reason for the shift toward kingship was just the general sociological shift among all the people groups of that time towards a centralised government which ancient Israel likewise followed. The people wanted a king to be like all the other nations. They also wanted a king to fight their battles for them. While it is the people who ask for a king in 1 Samuel 8, it does not seem to be a surprise to God.

According to the Old Testament, the development of kingship as a form of leadership or government was anticipated by God in Deuteronomy 17:14-20. The principles and guidelines for the anticipated king were outlined, including the criteria for selection and their functions – such as upholding the Levitical law. However as the history of the monarchy demonstrates, the kings did not always fulfil this duty. While ancient Israel drew heavily on the kingship model of the nations around them, it did not completely adopt this model but adapted it. Many of the surrounding nations of the ancient Near East considered their kings to be divine and so practised ruler worship (such as Pharaoh). In contrast, ancient Israel did not regard their kings to be divine. Instead they are presented in the Old Testament as very human. They are criticised and challenged by the prophets (see Isa 14:12-15; Ezek 28:2-10). However, there is a sense that the king is the divine choice and has special gifts (Ps 2:7).

The threat of the Philistines was a major issue to the ancient Israelites. It was also a threat to their faith. As demonstrated at the conquest of the land in Joshua, God is the powerful king who promised to protect his subjects from danger threatened by their enemies. Throughout the Old Testament writings the imagery of God's armies, and the title of God as the "Lord of Hosts", was evoked to remind people of the covenant protection provided by God.[16] This was particularly seen in one of the confrontations with the Philistines in 1 Samuel 17. This was the battle with the Philistine champion and giant, Goliath. The army of ancient Israel under Saul were currently at a stand-off. A battle between the entire armies could be avoided if one man was willing to fight Goliath. However no man was willing to confront this giant. No man was willing, except a teenager named David.

David was delivering cheese to his older brothers when he overheard the threats of this arrogant Philistine, Goliath. He volunteered to fight him - much to the aghast of his brothers and Saul. Yet he convinced them through the testimony of his exploits as a shepherd in protecting his sheep from bears and lions that he was the one for the job. He had experienced God's deliverance more than once. God could deliver him again. So armed only with his shepherd's sling, he confronted Goliath. As you read 1 Samuel 17: 45-47 you will notice that David evoked the name of the "Lord of Hosts". He said: "You come against me with sword and spear and javelin, but I come against you in the name of the Lord Almighty, the God of the armies of Israel, whom you have defied" (TNIV). He called on God as the divine warrior to fight for his behalf. God responded to his faith. Goliath and the Philistines were defeated.

Take a moment to consider the significance of this concept of the image of God using our tools of the trade. How is this passage significant to *them, us & me*? The significance of 1 Samuel 17: 45-47 may be demonstrated as:

The significance to *them* is:

- God delivered the people of ancient Israel from the threat of extermination by the Philistines (*represented by Goliath ready in battle*)

- Their warfare was fought over a physical, geographic territory using physical weapons (*represented by ancient weaponry and armoury*)

- God acted though the faith of David, who would later become king of ancient Israel (*represented by the boy David*)

- God had prepared David with gifts and abilities for this encounter (*represented by David's slingshot*)

- When the people called on the name of God, he delivered them. God acted no matter how impossible the situation seemed. This deliverance was God's fulfilment of covenant promise (*representation of God as the divine warrior*)

- God acts on their behalf in the unseen realm that impacts the physical realm (*representation of God as the divine warrior*)

The significance to *us* is:

- From this preserved family (*represented by the boy David*), Jesus Christ would come

- Jesus Christ is the ultimate representation of the divine warrior. This culminated at the cross where he defeated Satan not by killing but by dying. Col 2:14-15 understands the cross to be a great military victory. (*representation of God as the divine warrior*)

- The New Testament informs us that Jesus, the divine warrior, will appear again in the future to finalise the victory and rid the cosmos of Satan and all evil (*representation of God as the divine warrior*)

- We no longer fight for a physical territory. The object of our warfare has shifted from flesh-and-blood enemies to the spiritual powers that empower evil in the world (*representation of God as the divine warrior*)

Although this will be different for each reader, **the significance to *me* is:**

- God responds to faith (*represented by the boy David*)

- I may think I am just going about my daily duties (*like David delivering cheese*) but God is guiding my steps when I am obedient to him (*represented by the boy David*)

- The weaponry I use is spiritual, not physical (Eph 6:10-12). I fight in faith for the spiritual territory God has given me (*represented by the boy David*)

- God will equip me with gifts and abilities for the battles I face (*represented by David's slingshot*)

This boy, David, would eventually become king of ancient Israel. However the introduction of kingship into ancient Israel was a development. While 1 Samuel introduces the concept of kingship, we see that it was a process to get from charismatic leadership to administrative king. The first attempt was Saul. Saul was like the charismatic leaders of Judges. He was anointed not as a king, but as a chieftain.[17] Saul was less than a king, but more than a judge. He still functioned as a military leader. Like a judge, his military leadership was defensive only and drawn from a volunteer army. Saul did not introduce any governmental innovations. In this sense, Saul's role as chieftain was a link between the charismatic leadership of the judges and the dynastic kings. However some of the decisions of Saul disqualified him from the leadership of ancient Israel (see 1 Samuel 15). So, David was appointed. His rule over all ancient Israel and Judah was to last approximately 33 years. It was known as a golden era in the history of ancient Israel.

One of the most significant acts of King David was the capture of Jerusalem. David established Jerusalem (or Zion) as the political and spiritual capital of Israel. It was the ideal place for the capital as it was neutral ground between Judah (David's tribe) and the northern tribes (formerly loyal to Saul). King David was able for the first time to bring the land of promise completely under the control of ancient Israel. He subdued other nations in his offensive wars. His wars against the Philistines resulted in them never being a significant threat to ancient Israel ever again (5:17-25; 21:15-22). David centralised the administration of the whole nation. For example, he created a national taxation system, a permanent army through subscription and established political alliances. Through the conscription of services (such as builders and artisans) he built a royal palace and prepared the way for the building of the Temple in Jerusalem.[18] Ancient Israel was now the most powerful kingdom in western Asia, stretching from the river of Egypt in the south to the regions of the Euphrates (reminiscent of the promise given in Gen.15:18).[19]

However with David's great wealth and prestige came the seeds of later problems. He had numerous wives (2 Samuel 2:2; 3:2-5; 3:13-14; 11:26-27). While most of these marriages had political implications (they secured political treaties), polygamy was warned against in the Mosaic Law (Deut.17:17). The many children became the source of great rivalry and sin within the family. Yet, despite his many failings, David is upheld by the testimony of the Old Testament as the ultimate shepherd-king. He is the model by which all other kings were measured. Even when he failed, he returned to God in repentance (see 2 Samuel 12 and Psalm 51). Saul and David had been unexpectedly chosen by God and anointed by the Spirit. They were like charismatic rulers who ruled the previous generations. However this changed with the appointing of Solomon as the heir to the throne. With Solomon we see a new system of selection established called dynastic succession. This meant that the next rulers were not necessarily by direct divine appointment, but were the sons of the reigning king. It is one of the essential features of kingship as a model of leadership.

In particular, it would be the heirs of David that were the legitimate rulers of Judah. This was promised by God in 2 Sam.7:5-16. This is known as the 'Davidic covenant'. It was a formal commitment by God to establish David and his descendants on the throne. This promise was given when David asked Nathan the prophet for God's approval to build a temple for the Lord. But God refused David's request. God promised instead to make David a "house" (or a dynasty).[20] Although God would discipline or judge individual kings for their failures in office or obedience to God, his covenant loyalty would not be withdrawn from David's house (vv.14b-16). Yet, it still required their obedience (1 Kings 11:32-39; Ps 89). In this way, God designated the king from the line of David to be the messiah. The term 'messiah' means "anointed". It reflects the ancient practice of anointing or smearing a person with oil. It set apart a person for a particular office. In the Old Testament, when the term was used in royal contexts, it always referred to the reigning king.[21] The current king was the messiah, the anointed one. The current king was God's representative to rule on earth.

The later experiences of ancient Israel after the death of David, particularly the division and decline of the kingdom which will be discussed next, led to a hope that a messiah would come to restore ancient Israel to a position of prestige among the nations.[22] The hope that a Davidic king would come and bring the restitution of the full Davidic covenant was the foundation for the messianic theology of the prophets (Jer 33:14-26). Jesus is the fulfilment of that promise, but not in a way necessarily anticipated by Israel at the time of his ministry. This promise of a perpetual kingdom is ultimately a messianic prophecy of what God will do for the human race in the redemptive work of Christ.[23] In the New Testament, we continue the work of Christ by expanding the spiritual territory of his rule. The Holy Spirit is given to each of us to equip us for this task. The emphasis is not on the act of anointing, but on the Holy Spirit with whom we are anointed. It refers to the fact that we are all anointed – the Holy Spirit has come on all believers (Acts 2).

GROUP DISCUSSION QUESTIONS:

1. What has happened in the testimony of ancient Israel from creation up to this point (Davidic covenant)? In your group, make a time-line of the major events.

2. What are the differences between charismatic leadership and kingship (or monarchic leadership) in the Old Testament?

3. How is Jesus similar to the revelation of God as a warrior in the Old Testament?

4. Read Judges 4 (the story of Deborah). Apply the 'tools of the trade' to this passage:

    i. What is the significance to *them*?

    ii. What is the significance to *us*?

    iii. What is the significance to *me*?

RECOMMENDED READING

␬ Longman, Tremper. & Reid, Daniel G., *God is a Warrior*, (Grand Rapids, Michigan: Zondervan, 1995).

This is a great study on the theme of the divine warrior. It tracks the development of the theme through the entire Bible from the Pentateuch through to Revelation. It is very easy to read as well.

␬ Anderson, B.W., *The Living World of the Old Testament*, 4th Ed, (Essex: Longman, 1990)

Although this is a general to introduction to the Old Testament, Anderson's section on the rise of the monarchy is particularly excellent. It is a great resource to have.

ENDNOTES

1. Brueggemann, W., *The Covenanted Self*, (Minneapolis: Augsburg, 1999), p.99

2. Brueggemann, W., *The Land: Place as Gift, Promise, and Challenge in Biblical Faith*, 2nd Ed, (Minneapolis: Augsburg Fortress Press, 2002), p.46.

3. Brueggemann, W., *The Covenanted Self*, p.101.

4. Longman, T., *Making Sense of the Old Testament: Three Crucial Questions*, p.74.

5. Longman, T., *Making Sense of the Old Testament: Three Crucial Questions*, p74-76.

6. Longman, T., *Making Sense of the Old Testament: Three Crucial Questions*, p.76.

7. Longman ,T. & Reid, D.G., *God is a Warrior*, (Grand Rapids, Michigan: Zondervan, 1995), p.49

8. Longman, T., *Making Sense of the Old Testament: Three Crucial Questions*, p.72

9. Longman, T., *Making Sense of the Old Testament: Three Crucial Questions*, p.72

10. Longman T. & Reid, D.G., *God is a Warrior*, p.46

11. Brueggemann, W., *The Covenanted Self*, p.100

12. LaSor, W.S., Hubbard, D.A. & Bush, F.W., *Old Testament Survey: The Message, Form, and Background of the Old Testament*, 2nd Ed, p.148

13. LaSor, W.S., Hubbard, D.A. & Bush, F.W., *Old Testament Survey: The Message, Form, and Background of the Old Testament*, 2nd Ed, p.148

14. Charpentier, E., *How to Read the Bible: The Old and New Testaments*, p.18

15. Yee, G.A., 'By the Hand of a Woman: The Metaphor of the Woman Warrior in Judges 4', *Semeia*, No. 61, p.110

16 . Longman, T., *Making Sense of the Old Testament: Three Crucial Questions*, p.78

17. Anderson, B.W., *The Living World of the Old Testament*, 4th Ed, (Essex: Longman, 1990), p.215

18. LaSor, W.S., Hubbard, D.A. & Bush, F.W., *Old Testament Survey: The Message, Form, and Background of the Old Testament*, 2nd Ed, p.183-187

19. Anderson, B.W., *The Living World of the Old Testament*, 4th Ed, p.224

20. Anderson, B.W., *The Living World of the Old Testament*, 4th Ed, p.230

21. Anderson, B.W., *The Living World of the Old Testament*, 4th Ed, p,233

22. Anderson, B.W., *The Living World of the Old Testament*, 4th Ed, p.233

23. 'Covenant' in Ryken, L., Wilhoit, J.C. & Longman, T. (eds) *Dictionary of Biblical Imagery*, (Downers Grove: IVP, 1998), p. 178

Chapter 11

PROPHETS AND KINGS

Our last chapter left the testimony of ancient Israel with the establishment of kingship as the new form of government. This government united the tribes into a single nation led by King David and then his son Solomon. This was a 'golden period' of prosperity and wealth. However their unity proved superficial. The wealth was unevenly distributed. The court administrators and the upper classes grew more rich whilst the general population and peasantry grew more poor. The general population buckled under the weight of heavy taxes and conscription. In particular, the people of the northern areas resented their taxes and labour contributing to the wealth of the south. It was in southern Israel, particularly in Jerusalem, that the palace and a lot of the building projects were located. Yet, David had been taken from the sheep-folds and unexpectedly chosen by God for this role. So although he was from the southern tribe of Judah, David was basically tolerated as a ruler by the northerners. This is because he was one of the people. However his son Solomon, and subsequent rulers from the Davidic line, were raised in the palace and as a result were very removed from the people and the concerns of the public.

Like his father, Solomon started his rule well. His wisdom was renowned around the world. Even the legendary Queen of Sheba came to investigate his renowned wisdom (see 1 Kings 10; 2 Chronicles 9). During this time there was a surge of interest in literature and the arts. In particular, there was an increased interest in wisdom literature (of which Solomon was considered the patron), which will be explored in the next chapter. But toward the end of his reign, Solomon had brought religious corruption into the palace. This was generally due to his massive wealth and enormous number of wives. Although most of these wives would have been from political treaty arrangements, they were allowed to practice their own religions. This allowed idolatry and syncretism to creep into the palace - and into the heart of the king. So although he began as the wisest of kings, he ended his life a fool.[1] Solomon also continued to burden the people with extensive taxes (1 Kings 4:7, 22-28). The administration of them seems to have ignored the traditional tribal boundaries which created further resentment. There were also forced labour gangs created to build various public works (1 Kings 5:13-14). So while it seemed to be a 'golden age' of expansion and wealth, it proved to be shallow. Under the surface there were deep problems within the nation.

After the death of Solomon, the kingdom was torn apart and divided. When Solomon's heir (Rehoboam) came to the throne, the northern tribes demanded that the heavy burdens be made lighter. However Rehoboam rejected the advice of the older counsellors and accepted the words of the younger men who had grown up with him in the palace. His response to the ultimatum was recorded in 1 Kings 12:14, where Rehoboam says: "My father made your yoke heavy: I will make it even heavier. My father scourged you with whips; I will scourge you with scorpions" (TNIV). This sparked the explosion of all the pent-up anger of the northerners to the southern rulers. Their cry became:

"What portion have we in David?

We have no inheritance in the son of Jesse

To your tents, O Israel!

Look now to your own house, David." (1 Kings 12:16 TNIV)

This led to the division of the kingdom of ancient Israel. So from this time on, the nation was known as two separate groups. They formed two territories. The ten tribes of the north formed the northern kingdom (known as 'Israel' or 'Ephraim'). The tribes of Judah and some of Benjamin formed the southern kingdom (known as 'Judah'). So if a passage refers to 'Israel' it is important to check the context or date. If the passage refers to a time before the division, then it means the whole united kingdom of twelve tribes. If it is after the division (and before the exile) it refers to the northern kingdom. After the exile when only Judah remained, the biblical writers sometimes revert back to this original name of 'Israel' to give hope for the restoration of the nation and return to this golden era. This is very important to remember - particularly when reading the prophets - so you know who the biblical writers are referring to. It can be a bit confusing, but shows how a little bit of diligent research can add loads of meaning to your bible reading. However it is also essential to note that while the kingdom was divided into two separate political entities, they still recognised their common covenant relationship to God.

This revolt of the northerners was led by a slave called Jeroboam. He was portrayed negatively in these histories and became the archetype of an evil ruler. Throughout the book of Kings he was the standard of evil that the subsequent kings were measured against. His most abominable act was to create a new worship centre in the north at Bethel where he installed a re-constructed golden calf. This was a political attempt to shift the location and loyalty of worship away from Jerusalem (in the south) to a local centre in the north (1 Kings 12:25-33). The book of Kings constantly reminds readers of the wickedness of Jeroboam. As we discussed in chapter 5, this emphasises to contemporary readers that the biblical writers were not writing modern history, but a theological testimony. In their testimony, each northern and southern king was strictly examined. They were measured positively against David (for Judah) or negatively against Jeroboam (for Israel). A good example of this is found in 1 Kings 15- 16:7. The theological purpose of the biblical writers was to show the decline of the nation into sin and therefore exile.

The writers understood the two nations to be in covenant relationship with God. Their testimony shows that when the people were faithful to their covenant (as exemplified by the king), then the nation was blessed. When they were unfaithful, they were cursed. The decline of the people into idolatry showed they had violated the covenant. The ultimate curse of this idolatry would be their removal from the land into exile. This is the event to which the testimony of these books points. It offers an explanation of how and why the exile came about. Theologically, they intend to show that their decline and exile did not happen by chance. It was by the decree of God. This is also why there are some prophetic oracles woven into the testimony. The historical writings contain some words of the prophets woven into their testimony (such as Elijah). Other words of the prophets (such as Isaiah and Hosea) are recorded as separate books, but they were active during this time before the exile. Some of the prophets (such as Malachi and Joel) were active after the exile. This is because the history of ancient Israel was considered not just political, but dependent on God. If the people violated the covenant, they would receive the judgement of God. If they were obedient to covenant, they would be blessed. Their testimony shows that they chose judgement.

The history of the divided kingdom is described in the books of Kings and Chronicles. Of the two kingdoms of the north and south, the most politically stable was the south, Judah. It was stabilised by the dynasty of David. The Davidic covenant had identified the heirs of David to be the legitimate rulers. They remained on the throne in Jerusalem until the Babylonian Exile in 587BCE. However, the northern kingdom had a cycle of kings and a cycle of dynasties. This lack of a legitimate ruler led to great difficulties. Who was eligible to be a leader? When there was political confusion there would emerge a military leader who would restore stability and establish a dynasty. This military leader would usually lead a coup against the reigning family and establish a new dynasty. They were like the charismatic leader of the Judges period who would rise up in a time of crisis.

However, none of their dynasties tended to last for very long. This meant there was little stability. Of these northern kings, 8 out of 19 were assassinated. There was continual political intrigue. New and different new dynasties followed one after another. This meant that politically, it was very unstable. It was also during this time that the prophets were active. So the words of Hosea, Amos and Micah addressed the northern kingdom before its exile warning them of impending judgement. Although the kings themselves were no better or worse than the kings in the south, there was no real sense of legitimacy as to who could be king. As the prophet Hosea complained: "They made kings, but not by me" (Hosea 8:4 TNIV). Coupled with this political chaos was their fall into idolatry. They intermarried with the other nations who brought their gods into ancient Israel. A prime example of this in the north was the political marriage of the Phoenician princess, Jezebel, with King Ahab (1 Kings 16:29-34).

Throughout this period of the kings, there emerged the unique ministry of the prophets. Prophetic figures were existent in the history of ancient Israel prior to the development of the monarchy with leaders such as Moses and Deborah. However with the institution of the monarchy there was a shift. The prophet was foremost called to represent God to the king. They were God's spokesperson. That was their primary role. Because they were speaking on behalf of God they would often begin with the statement: "Thus says the Lord". This made it clear who was the originator of the message: God. The prophets were not always like itinerant preachers who moved from town to town. Neither did they necessarily target the general population. Instead, their primary role was to call ancient Israel's leadership to accountability. Their subject matter often involved the future of the nation – particularly if that future was in threat by the current policies or practices of the ruling king. During the monarchic period, sometimes the prophets would speak from within the king's court, such as Nathan or Isaiah. They were court prophets and would often act as a political consultant.

Sometimes the prophets stood outside the power structure as a critic, such as Elijah speaking to King Ahab. The prophets reminded the leadership of their covenant obligations.

Our journey through the testimony of ancient Israel so far has highlighted that the people were not always obedient to the laws or fulfilled their covenant requirements. So when the people forgot or neglected their covenant relationship, God used the prophets to remind the people of their covenant agreement. They were what Fee and Stuart call "covenant-enforcers".[2] They were covenant-enforcers because God announced the enforcement of the covenant (whether good or bad) through the prophets in the Old Testament. This connection to the covenant is important when reading the prophets. The blessings and curses that they uttered were not randomly invented. As Fee and Stuart note, they didn't just make up their speeches.[3] Their words were based on the promised result of the people's relationship to God. They were promised blessing if they obeyed the covenant or curses if they didn't. Through the prophets, God announced his intention to enforce the covenant, for benefit or harm, depending on the faithfulness of ancient Israel.[4] While the prophets are sometimes considered radical social reformers (because they often charged the rich with exploiting the poor and widowed), the charges they brought were already revealed in the covenantal law. They didn't present new ideas, but reminders of the law. However they often presented this 'old' information in startling new ways and images.[5]

Although the prophets were speaking to different groups at different times within the Old Testament, they were enforcing the same central covenant made at Sinai. At Sinai the people entered into covenant relationship with God and were bound to abide by the covenant rules established at that time. These rules, the laws, did not change. The people were bound to them because they were in covenant. The prophets spoke to the people to remind them of their responsibility to abide by that covenant. They wanted their theology (what they believed) to match their practice (what they did). This is a good guideline for all believers! Yet, because of the failure of the people to obey the covenant, much of what appears in the prophetic books are warnings of the negative consequences of failing to obey. Time and time again through the prophets, God warned the people of the curses he would be required to enforce, hoping for signs of repentance from the people.

Because the prophets were engaged as covenant-enforcers (which refers to a legally binding treaty) it is not surprising that they often used legal language in their messages. The prophets were sent by God to 'present' the case of God against ancient Israel. Consider, for example, Micah 6:1-8. In this presentation, Micah acts like a covenant lawyer as he gives the charges levelled against the people. He uses legal language, style, and imagery to charge the people of their neglect. It is the same message of the Sinai covenant, but it is presented differently. If the people heard the same message over and over again, they would not listen. So his presentation was aimed to captivate the listeners with its freshness and originality. They would often use poetry to express their message.

Let's consider the significance of this passage of Micah 6:1-8 using the tools of our trade. How is this passage significant to *them, us & me*?

The significance to *them* is:

- The prophet is the spokesperson of God. The prophet speaks through the language of poetry

- God is reminding the people of their covenant relationship and obligations which they are rejecting. God is calling the Northern Kingdom before their exile to return to the heart of their covenant

- Because it is a legal agreement the prophet speaks to them like a lawyer. The original witness to this agreement between God and ancient Israel was creation (for example, Joshua 24:27). Micah calls on the witnesses in verse 1-2

- God reminds them of their history of relationship (verse 4-5). God rescued them from Egypt. God saved them from the curses and attacks of the other nations

- The prophet reminds the people that their covenant is about relationship and not going through the motions to pretend obedience. In this sense, no sacrifice (not even their "firstborn" child) is good enough if it is not from the heart

- The prophet summarises the heart of the law and its relationship with God in verse 8. The heart of the law is for them to walk humbly before God. This relationship would then flow out to their actions of justice and mercy. They are to love God and to reflect his character

The significance to *us* is:

- Jesus Christ came from this people of ancient Israel

- Where ancient Israel failed to be obedient, Jesus Christ fulfilled the role

- Jesus Christ, described as the firstborn of the Father, was given to restore this lost relationship of humanity with God

- Jesus Christ inaugurates a new way of life and worship for the people of God in the New Testament. Although the sacrificial system has been displaced, the heart of the covenant is still the same. We are still required to walk humbly before God. This relationship should then flow out to our actions of justice and mercy. We are to love God and to reflect his character.

Although this will be different for each reader, **the significance to me** is:

- I can work for God and dedicate my life (as a living offering) to do all sorts of activity to please God. However, in the end, working for God does not mean that I love God. What God requires of me is actually very simple. When we strip away all the activity, it is about loving God and walking humbly before him. Then whatever activities I do to demonstrate my love flow out of that relationship. Works are an expression of gratitude and devotion, not a way to win God's heart

As God's spokesperson, the prophet stood above the king in spiritual authority. They would often bring a challenge or guidance on behalf of God to the ruler. However politically, they were subject to the mercy of the king. This made them vulnerable to persecution (such as Jeremiah). Because of their authority, we often have the birth narratives of the prophets in the Old Testament and not the kings. Their birth narrative was often linked to their calling. They were chosen from birth for this vocation. The call of the prophet (such as Jeremiah 1:4–10 and Ezekiel 2:1–7) is important for several reasons. It confirms the appointment of the prophet for their own benefit, as well as the benefit of their society. Even though many of the prophets expressed their inadequacy, or reluctance to take up the task, they were God's choice. So if you have ever felt inadequate to perform a task for God, you are not alone! Their experience of God affirmed them and identified themselves as messengers - even if the people rejected their message. Jeremiah claims that the false prophets had not been called (Jer 14:14), and later stresses that the false prophets had not "stood in the council of the Lord" (Jer 23:18 TNIV).

Let's take for example, the call of Isaiah (Is 6: 1-9). It presents a vision of Isaiah's calling to the prophetic ministry. He had an immediate and direct experience of God's holiness through a vision of the throne room of the "Lord of Hosts". In this throne room, the heavenly King was presiding even though the earthly king (Uzziah) had died. The vision was of both beauty and terror. Overwhelmed by God's holiness,[6] the prophet recognised his own un-holiness. He recognised not only his personal uncleanness, but the inadequacy of the Judean community he represented. Having this purged, the prophet received a message of judgement for the community. The experience authorised the prophet and legitimated his message. The authority attributed to the prophet to speak to the people came from this encounter with God.

However these passages from Isaiah 6 and Micah 6 show us that following the covenant wasn't just about following the letter of the law. The heart of the covenant was relationship with God. The heart of it was for the people to reflect God. The prophets understood God. They had a revelation of God as possessing certain moral features. They perceived God's character to be holy, good and perfect. And because God is understood to be holy, the prophets thought that this standard should be reflected in the lives of the followers of God. If God is holy, then surely the followers of God should also be holy. So Isaiah at the time of his call encountered the holy God in the sanctuary. This encounter came to dominate his whole preaching. It informed his understanding of God. It also characterised how he thought the people should respond to God. If God is holy, then God's followers should reflect this holiness in their social lives, politics and economic practices. The prophet sought to challenge the people to reflect their God (as vassals were meant to). For Micah, God was revealed as a lover of justice. If God is just, then the people (God's worshippers) should also be just. The personal experiences of the prophets were regarded as of paramount importance. It was through such experiences that the prophets were able to understand certain truths about the nature of God and the requirements of his people.

However there is often confusion among contemporary readers over the nature of prophecy in the Old Testament. Many current readers would consider prophecy to be fore-telling. That is, its purpose is to predict future events or what is to come. So many Christian readers only value the Old Testament prophets because they predict the coming of Christ. According to Fee and Stuart, less than two percent of Old Testament prophecy is actually messianic. Less than one percent concerns events yet to come.[7] This does not mean that we can't see Christ in many of the prophetic writings, but that was not necessarily their original purpose. The prophets did announce the future. However they were announcing the immediate future of ancient Israel rather than our future.[8] The purpose of God in speaking through a prophet was not to communicate information about the distant future, but to speak to the current generation with a message for them. God speaks to people where they were at. The words of the prophets were the words of rebuke, challenge, comfort or encouragement to their generation. Although they often give us hints about Jesus, we must honour their words as God speaking to *them*. The prophets were not just fore-tellers, but forth-tellers.

The words of the prophets were meant to be relevant to their contemporary audience. If they just spoke words about the distant future that had no relevance to their community then their words would be empty. Instead, their message was important and directly relevant to their listeners. However this does not mean that they didn't announce future events. To understand this phenomenon, Anderson likens it to a doctor's prediction that a patient has only a short time to live. This prediction (or diagnosis) makes the patient's present moments more precious and serious. This prophetic announcement of what God was about to do also emphasised the urgency of the present moment to the immediate generation. In this way, perhaps the patient through medication or changes in lifestyle could change the prediction of the doctor. So also the people at the time of the prophet could change the prophetic announcement if necessary.[9] The purpose of it was to elicit a response. The judgement of the prophets was intended to turn the people to repentance and worship. Although sometimes the prophets did predict the future, it was given as a warning of the results of disobedience and hope for the future. We see this happening in the book of Jonah. Jonah was sent outside of ancient Israel to the city of Nineveh with a pronouncement of judgement and coming doom. The people responded in repentance and judgement was avoided. So the message of Jonah was clearly aimed at his contemporary audience.

This example of Jonah reminds us of an important point in the study of prophecy generally. The concept of 'prophet' and 'prophecy' was not unique to ancient Israel. As Ben Witherington notes, almost all of the ancient cultures had people who exercised roles that we would call prophetic.[10] The prophets of ancient Israel, or even of the New Testament, did not operate in a cultural vacuum. That is why Jonah, or Balaam, or the Apostle Paul could step over geographical and cultural boundaries and still be recognised as a sort of prophetic figure. The forms and roles were the same throughout this time and region. This is also seen in the confrontation of Elijah with the prophets of Ba'al who had been introduced by Jezebel (1 Kings 18: 16-46). The role and function of the prophets of Ba'al were similar to the role and function of prophets in ancient Israel. However Elijah's showdown on Mt Carmel demonstrates that the prophets of ancient Israel spoke on behalf of the one true God.

Because the prophets were forth-tellers, God used them to speak to the people using images and language familiar to them. God spoke to them where they were at. So the words of the prophets were mainly recorded as poetry. Their words were vivid and easily remembered for an oral society. For example, Isaiah 5: 1-7 uses the familiar image of the vineyard. It is interesting to note that the prophet was charging the people with neglect of the covenant. God gave them all that was necessary to live as his people, but they rejected the covenant and became the "wild grapes". They had everything they needed (such as the law and the prophets) to produce the fruit of righteousness. Instead they produced bloodshed and death. The prophet presents this in a powerful way that we completely miss in our English translations but is clear in the Hebrew. God looked for justice (*mishpat*) from the people but found only bloodshed (*mispach*).[11]   Instead of righteousness (*sedaqa*) he heard cries of distress (*se'aqa*).[12]   These words sound very similar in the Hebrew but have totally different meanings. The prophet gave this demand for social justice as a basic covenant obligation. Because the leaders failed this, the result would be judgement. The prophets generally used images and metaphors familiar to the life of their audience.

Yet, why would the prophet use the image of a vineyard and not another image, such as a kangaroo farm? Wine was an essential part of the diet of the ancient world. In particular, the land of Judah was full of vineyards, not kangaroos. It was a common crop. It was used at this time to pay for the luxury goods imported into Judah by the elite minority. So it is not surprising that the vine and the vineyard would serve as a powerful image for the people. Wine also represented the latest innovations and technology. There is quite a lot of archaeological evidence indicating a surge in technology at this time in the eighth century for increased production of wine.[13] In particular there was an increase in innovative equipment regarding the protection and processing of the grapes (like the winepress and tower mentioned in v.2). So the owner of the vineyard is like one of the rich elite who has acquired land off a poor peasant and has now planted a vineyard with all the latest innovations. They are expecting this technology to produce a substantial crop to trade for luxury items.

From this study of the social and historical context, we can see that the vineyard was a proud symbol of economic progress and prosperity. But perhaps to the peasants and the poor, the vineyard represented their injustice. So the 'vineyard' was not a neutral word or image used by Isaiah. Neither is the choice of the song. Who according to Isaiah 5:12 listens to songs? It was the rich who sat up all night with harps and lyres at their banquets. It was the unjust, rich rulers who were listening to the songs. This was the audience that Isaiah was addressing. So the form (style of writing) is suited to the audience. The New Testament also continues the use of the vineyard imagery, but with a twist. It is not just ethnic Israel that is the vineyard, but the people of God. As Christian believers, we have been grafted into the vineyard of God's people.

It is crucial for contemporary readers in making sense of Old Testament prophecy, to put it into some kind of context in the history or testimony of God's plan of salvation. The prophets spoke to people about the events they were witnessing in their own lifetime. God spoke to people where they were at, in ways they could understand (their own language). Yet, being 'called' as a prophet implies that others were *not* called. In other words, it was a special role that only a select few or 'special' people could fill. Only a small number of people were called as prophets to be the spokespeople of God. During the ministry of Jesus Christ he promised a radical change to this – he promised the Holy Spirit (Acts 1). It was not until the Day of Pentecost (Acts 2) that we could see this role revolutionised. For the post-Pentecost people of God, all who receive the Spirit can prophesy. We can all participate in this noble task of speaking on behalf of God to remind one another of the covenant we have with Jesus Christ. Yet, what is this new covenant that we enforce? Before the new covenant established by Christ, the people of God only had the Sinai covenant (which they continually disregarded). Yet their testimony is recorded for us to show both the faithfulness and justice of God. However, as Christian readers, we now live under the new covenant. Like ancient Israel we are also required to be faithful to this covenant and the stipulations. Our new covenant is founded in Christ. It requires us to simply love God and each other. Yet, this is not so simple in practice! So we can learn a lot from the Old Testament community about the importance of being faithful to our covenant with God. We can also learn a lot from the Old Testament community about the nature and character of God whom we love.

So the prophets warned of the coming judgement. If the people continued to violate their covenant, then the justice of God would require their punishment. Throughout this time in the wider ancient Near Eastern world, there was an emerging super-power,

Assyria. While the influence of Egypt was declining, the muscle of Assyria was rising. They wanted to extend their power to the prosperous sea ports. This led them into direct conflict with the nations in the Fertile Crescent, particularly Damascus, Syria, Israel (north) and Judah (south). It was this nation of Assyria that God would use as the tool of his punishment. Assyria would be the means of God's punishment of his people. Eventually, Assyria marched on Israel (north) and slowly chipped away at the kingdom. This left only the capital Samaria besieged. So Hoshea, king of Israel made a treaty and became a vassal to Assyria. The Assyrian king had decimated Israel but did not overthrow the capital of Samaria. They continued to receive their tribute money.

The smaller nations of the Palestinian area, mainly Syria and Israel, formed a coalition to rebel against the Assyrian Empire. This was called the Syro-Ephraimite War of 733BC. They wanted to throw off the shackles of Assyria as the ruling power in the ancient Near East. However, while the northern kingdom was at the centre of the rebellion against Assyrian domination, the southern kingdom refused. So this coalition turned against the southern king Ahaz in the hope of replacing him with a ruler more sympathetic to their aims. The southern kingdom was under threat, and betrayed by the northern kingdom. Isaiah prophesied that the Syro-Israelite alliance would fail. In Isaiah 7:4 the prophet says: "Do not loose heart because of these two smouldering stubs of firewood". He goes on to say in verse 7: "the Sovereign Lord says: "It will not take place, it will not happen"" (TNIV). And the confirmation that the siege would fail is a promised "sign". The sign promised is the birth of a child whose name would be called Immanuel (Is 7:14). The sign is that even before the child reaches the age of choosing between good and evil, the alliance would have broken up (8:1-4). This was a message to their generation that was fulfilled in their generation. It also speaks to us of the birth of Christ.

However Ahaz did not listen to the words or take notice of the sign of Isaiah. It seemed that without faith in the prophetic word of God, that he had two choices. He could either surrender to the Syro-Israelite alliance. By doing this he would probably loose his throne, and also risk being on the wrong side of Assyria.[14] Or he could call upon Assyria and basically submit to being their vassal. So Ahaz chose to become a vassal of Assyria. Assyria came, broke up the siege and later attacked the northern kingdom for their rebellion. The northern king, Hoshea, looked to Egypt for help. However Egypt was too weak to save them. Samaria fell to Assyria in about 721BCE after a three-year siege. So northern Israel went into exile. While most of the inhabitants were deported, a large number remained in the capital of Samaria. The Assyrians also brought colonists to Samaria from other provinces of their empire, including Babylonians. From this group, a new population was created. They were considered by the Judeans to be of mixed blood. By the time of Jesus, they were known as the Samaritans. All this was seen as a result of northern Israel's unfaithfulness to the Mosaic covenant. So while the northern tribe fell to the Assyrian blitz which extended through Palestine to the borders of Egypt, this left the southern kingdom of Judah a vassal of Assyria and very much alone. The destiny of the southern kingdom will be explored in chapter 13. But now we will turn to another aspect of ancient Israel's testimony, that is, their prayer, hymns, laments and wisdom literature.

GROUP DISCUSSION QUESTIONS:

1. What was the purpose of the Old Testament prophets?

2. What differences exist between prophets and kings?

3. How effective were the prophets?

4. Read Isaiah 5: 1-7. Apply the 'tools of the trade' to this passage:

    i. What is the significance to *them*?

    ii. What is the significance to *us*?

    iii. What is the significance to *me*?

RECOMMENDED READING

❧ Green, Joel B., *How to Read Prophecy*, (Leicester: IVP, 1984)

This is an excellent introduction to prophecy in the bible. It is easy to read and insightful.

❧ Webb, B., *The Message of Isaiah*, BST, (IVP, 1996)

This is a great little commentary if you want to go deeper into the book of Isaiah. Commentaries are an excellent source of guidance in reading.

❧ Witherington, Ben, *Jesus the Seer: The Progress of Prophecy*, (Massachusetts: Hendrickson, 1999)

This is quite a heavy book, but it is thorough. It outlines the understanding of the role of the prophet from the Old Testament to the time of Jesus. It also includes information of the wider cultural phenomenon of prophecy that impacted both ancient Israel and the early church.

ENDNOTES

1. Longman, T., *Making Sense of the Old Testament: Three Crucial Questions*, (Grand Rapids, Michigan: Baker, 1998), p.

2. Fee, G. D., & Stuart, D., *How to Read the Bible For all its Worth*, 3rd Ed., (Grand Rapids: Zondervan, 2003), p.184

3. Fee, G. D., & Stuart, D., *How to Read the Bible For all its Worth*, 3rd Ed., (Grand Rapids: Zondervan, 2003), p.187

4. Fee, G. D., & Stuart, D., *How to Read the Bible For all its Worth*, 3rd Ed.,

(Grand Rapids: Zondervan, 2003), p.184

5. Fee, G. D., & Stuart, D., *How to Read the Bible For all its Worth*, 3rd Ed., (Grand Rapids: Zondervan, 2003), p.187

6. Brueggemann, W., *Isaiah 1-39*, WBC, (Louisville: Westminster/John Knox Press, 1998), p.57

7. Fee, G. D., & Stuart, D., *How to Read the Bible For all its Worth*, 3rd Ed., (Grand Rapids: Zondervan, 2003), p.182

8. Fee, G. D., & Stuart, D., *How to Read the Bible For all its Worth*, 3rd Ed., (Grand Rapids: Zondervan, 2003), p.182

9. Anderson, B.W., *The Living World of the Old Testament*, 4th Ed, (Essex: Longman, 1990), p190.

10. Witherington, B. III, *Jesus the Seer: The Progress of Prophecy*, (Massachusetts: Hendrickson, 1999), p.8

11. These are pronounced as *mish-pat* and *mish-pakh*.

12. These are pronounced as *sed-a-car* and *se-a-car*.

13. Premnath, D.N., *Eighth Century Prophets: A Social Analysis*, (St. Louis, Missouri: Chalis Press), pp.58-62.

14. Anderson, B.W., *The Living World of the Old Testament*, 4th Ed, p.335

Chapter 12

The Psalms and Wisdom of ancient Israel

One of the most interesting aspects of the Old Testament is the diversity of writings and styles that it contains. As we noted in chapter 5, there is a multitude of different writing styles and genres. For example, we find among its pages both historical narratives and prophetic oracles - which we looked at in the last chapter. These different writing styles were very important to the ancient community, and conveyed crucial messages regarding their faith. However, probably the most dominant genre (apart from narrative) is poetry. In fact, if you took all of the poetry in the Old Testament, it is still longer than all the writings in the entire New Testament. So poetry is especially important for our understanding of God. We have noted previously that the style of poetry is marked by imagery. It uses literary devices such as metaphor and simile. It is not as relaxing to read as narrative. It makes you think! It presents ideas compressed into short, terse lines. Poetry speaks through images that are inexact and sometimes vague. So why would God speak to us through poetry? Poetry reminds us that the bible is not just an information book. Neither is it a self development book. This is important as we begin to look at the Psalms and wisdom literature. Although these writings can impart information and help us develop character and skills, this is not their primary purpose. The bible is a testimony to the faith of the people of God. So poetry is important to our faith. Why? Poetry is important because, as Tremper Longman notes, it appeals to the whole person. Poetry not only informs our intellects but it appeals to our wills, stirs our hearts, and stimulates our imagination.[1] Poetry speaks to us through the imagination.

As we have noted, the one of the main features of Hebrew poetry is its use of imagery. Images are word pictures. We don't understand poems to be literal. When we read in Psalm 18:2 that "The Lord is my rock, my fortress and my deliverer", we don't understand it to be literal. God is not literally a rock. Images work by comparison. They describe what is unknown by attributes or pictures that are known to us in our context. We understand God (unknown) through the comparison of the rock (known). We know that a rock (in any context) is solid, firm and a great foundation. Through this comparison I can know something of God. So I recognise through this image that God is solid, firm and a great foundation on which to build my life. The ability to interpret poetry is crucial for reading the bible, because almost every book includes some figurative language.

Often the Old Testament draws on images that are stereotypical. They are conventional images drawn from the culture and tradition of ancient Israel. They also often reflect the wider culture of the ancient Near East. These images were deeply entrenched in their culture (such as shepherds and vineyards). We also have these types of images in our culture. For example, in modern Western culture we have adopted stereotypical images for Christmas that are recognisable in the mainstream society. The secular image is, of course, Santa Claus. Santa is a large, jolly man dressed in red. He has a big white beard. He rides a sleigh pulled by reindeer, yelling "Ho Ho Ho". Santa Claus makes his entry down a chimney with a sack full of toys on his back, and leaves them under the Christmas tree.[2] If we try and 'modernise' or amend this image in our culture, it just doesn't work. Santa cannot have a goatee, be slim, wear green, or drive a mini-van. He cannot just leave the toys on the front door step. A deviation may be tolerated as part of a cartoon or humorous twist, but the twist only works because the standard picture is so well-known.

In the same way, the Old Testament poets used similar stereotypical language (though not of course, Santa Claus). While we have our own images, the culture of the ancient Near Eastern world had its own standard pictures that were well-known. So the image of God as a warrior was very well-known. When God appears in battle, it is fairly standard language that is used. Consider for a moment the passage of Psalm 97:1-6. This Psalm presents a picture of God marching down to earth in a spectacular form. He is accompanied by storms, dark clouds and thunder, lightning and heavy rain. This is important language that we often miss as modern readers. When God appears, creation cannot contain his presence. So when God is around, there is always phenomenon such as thunder, lightning, and the moon turning to blood.[3] His appearance affects the cosmos as the earth quakes and the Lord's enemies melt in fear or run away. This was a standard way to describe the gods in ancient Near Eastern poetry. The poets and prophets generally used images and metaphors familiar to the life of their audience (like vineyards), but may not be as familiar to us. So we must understand what the image means in the culture and then translate that image to our world. We don't just 'cut and paste' the image to our culture or we may completely misunderstand the message.

By reading this passage of Psalm 97, we see that the images are not just flowery language. This is a common misperception when reading poetry. Particularly Aristotle thought that metaphors were just embellishments or decorations to make the speaker sound clever.[4] Actually, the use of metaphor and imagery is more than just decorations. An image expresses what cannot be said directly. If it could be said directly, then they would say it. But it cannot. We see this particularly in describing God. Take a moment to think: how would you describe God? Have you seen him? What does he look like? Is he, say, six foot tall with dark-ish, light-ish hair? For a people that cannot see God or do not know God, how does the Old Testament describe him? In one sense, God is indescribable. We cannot describe this almighty, creator, redeemer, judge, faithful…. Being?

If we could say it directly, then we would. But it is difficult. Imagery then, as Sally McFague writes, becomes a strategy of desperation, not decoration.[5] It is an attempt to say something of the unfamiliar in terms of the familiar. It is an attempt to speak about what we do not know in terms of what we do know. Even the prophet in Isaiah 40:25 says: "To whom, then, can you compare me; To whom can I be likened – says the Holy One." This is ironic because God cannot be compared to anything. Yet, in the desperation to understand God, we must compare God to things and relationships we understand. It is an attempt to describe the indescribable. Poetry helps us to do this.

So you have probably already noticed that the bible uses a lot of different images to describe God. This tells us that one single image is not enough. We cannot encapsulate God in one word. We need all the images and metaphors to help our human minds understand our awesome God.[6] The use of metaphor recognises that its description is partial. God is like a shepherd, but that is not all that God is. To speak of God as a shepherd is to consider some qualities of a shepherd that highlight aspects of God's relationship with us. But we also inherently recognise that the description is not enough. God does not just act like a shepherd – he is much more. This also means that no single metaphor or image will be enough to describe God. Since no one metaphor or image refers properly or directly to God, many are necessary. Different metaphors emphasise different aspects of God, so all are important. So, even though the images used by the bible are partial and inadequate, they are also desperately needed.[7]

Sometimes, an image or metaphor will create something new. It will inspire a new understanding of who God is and how God operates within our world.[8] This is what poetry does. It inspires (through images), new ways of understanding God. It can do this by using images that we do not expect. This forces us to make connections we do not anticipate. We are forced to ponder the unexpected image. For example, the imagery of Psalm 27:1

compares God to a light. It says: "The Lord is my light and my salvation; Whom shall I fear?" Perhaps this comparison can actually transform our understanding. Maybe our understanding of light is transformed by the comparison with God. Somehow light is more transcendent, life-giving and appreciated. Maybe God seems more warm, or golden or clear or even readily available everywhere (as light is). So the concepts are transformed by the comparison.

Another startling image is presented in Psalm 78:65: "Then the Lord awoke as from sleep, as a man wakes from the stupor of wine" (TNIV). This is quite a shocking image! God is compared to a man who has awoken from sleep. But this is not just any sleep. It is the sleep of a drunkard. In other words, like someone with a 'hangover'. What is someone like who has a hang-over? They're cranky, they've got a headache, and they're short-tempered.[9] This is what God is like in this situation. It is not suggesting that God literally has a hangover. However God in this situation of Psalm 78 acts like a head-sore man. God has awoken to re-claim his people. This image challenges us to think about God in ways we have never considered. Yet while this image reveals something of God, it also conceals. While God may act like a drunken man, God is not a drunken man. The image still does not fully reveal who God is. In a sense, this ambiguity protects the mystery of God from becoming mundane. Poetry reveals yet conceals. So why not just say it as it is? Whereas it would takes pages to communicate all these things that God is to us. Imagery says it in a profound and compact way. It also forces us to think, ponder, imagine and act.

Another way that poetry forces us to reflect and ponder the words more closely is the literary technique of parallelism. We have mentioned previously a little bit about this literary device. Parallelism is two lines of poetry side by side. They are parallel. But it's not just any two lines side by side. It is two lines that are connected. Usually these lines are trying to express the same point. Often it will say the same thing in two different ways. At first glance, it may seem that

the Psalms are needlessly repetitive. However when we understand
the nature and use of poetry, we can see it is giving great insight into
the concepts it describes.[10] Consider the following lines from Psalm
2:1:

(A) Why do the nations conspire

(B) and the peoples plot in vain?

This is an example of what is called 'synonymous' parallelism. These
two lines are not trying to say two different things.[11] When you look
at it closely, you will notice that the second line (B) basically says the
same thing as the first line (A). However, it says it in a different way.
In the first line it refers to "the nations" (A) while in the second line
it refers to "the peoples" (B). This is really the same thing, except
worded differently. It is in parallel. It's almost like an echo. It doesn't
mean that the "peoples" are every living being while the "nations"
are different. The peoples and the nations are doing the same thing
in this Psalm. However it is not written twice because the writer
loves to hear their own voice. Parallelism sharpens the thought.[12]
It intensifies the idea that is being expressed. It can be compared
to hammering a nail into a wall. In two quick movements the first
hit of the hammer secures the nail while the second blow hammers
it home. Consider again Psalm 2:1. What is different in these two
lines? The idea of their conspiracy against God (A) is sharpened in
definition by the recognition of their plotting (B). They are not just
scheming, but acting upon that evil scheme. This is not passive talk,
they are taking action. How does the second line intensify the first?
It tells us that their plotting is in vain. They are like the builders of
the tower of Babel, vainly trying to out-smart God. Yet their task is
futile, because God Almighty is the true king.

There is another type of parallelism. It is called 'antithetical
parallelism'. This is where the second line (B) restates the first line
(A) as a contrast. For example, Proverbs 10:1 says:

(A) Wise children bring joy to their fathers,

(B) But the foolish bring grief to their mothers.

What are the two lines in this verse doing? They are saying the same thing, except through contrast. It doesn't mean that a mother doesn't care if a child is wise and a father is indifferent to a foolish child.[13] Instead, the second line restates the first line as a contrast. It highlights the central point of the verses.

Understanding the poetic devices used in the poetry of the Old Testament helps us to understand the message it presents. It reminds us that reading the bible is not just an intellectual exercise. Poetry appeals to the whole person. It not only informs our intellects but it appeals to our wills and stimulates our imagination. This is important because the bible recognises that we are holistic beings. We are not machines. We are people with feelings, hearts, wills, bodies, spirits, and needs. These needs are economic, physical, emotional and spiritual. Our spirituality cannot afford to neglect our whole selves. The bible addresses these neglected areas through the poetry in its pages. As we communicate God's word, we cannot neglect the power of words and particularly the power of poetry. Probably the most powerful poetry we have in the Bible is found in the Book of Psalms.

So far in our journey, we have heard the testimony of ancient Israel. The Psalms continue that testimony as they record the prayers, songs and worship of ancient Israel. The Psalms provide a testimony of us humans speaking to or about God.[14] There are two metaphors that have been used in the history of the Christian church to describe the book of Psalms. The first metaphor is a garden. This was used by Martin Luther. He compared the book of Psalms to a garden. This emphasises the wild beauty and the many varieties of poetry that comprise the book. The book of Psalms has 150 poems of different lengths and different authors. They were written at different times, and contain different styles of poetry. The poems are like a multitude of different plants and flowers in a garden that bring delight to the observer, or reader.[15] The second metaphor used to describe the book of Psalms is a mirror. This was used by John Calvin. Reading the Psalms, you identify with the feelings and emotions of the writers. You associate yourself with their situation. In this sense, they become like a mirror to your own soul.

Let's consider this concept of the Psalms as a mirror a little more closely. Some scholars, such as Walter Brueggemann, compare the Psalms to the patterns of life and our response to the cycles of change.[16] Our lives are in constant change. Like the calendar year, our lives go through different seasons. We may be in a season of contentedness or pain or struggle. The Psalms help us to identify our current situation. But not only that, the Psalms then can help us to verbalise (through its imagery) what we are facing and thinking. They give us words to connect. Brueggemann calls these stages orientation, dis-orientation, and re-orientation. He categorises each of the psalms as representing these stages in a person's walk.[17] This model helps us to recognise why some psalms will appeal to us more than others. This is because we are at different stages in our walk. The psalms of different stages will appeal to us more because we resonant with the place or state that they represent. In this way the psalms are also a mirror because they reflect these stages of our life and walk with God. It is a great way to help you get the most out of the book of Psalms. Let's look at these three stages.

The stage of orientation is a state of contentedness. This is the sense that everything is in its place.[18] This can be a season in life – where we look around, and all is well. Everything is orientated in the right direction. Life is ordered. If we were hiking or sailing then this stage means that we are on course and going the right direction. It doesn't mean everything is perfect or we don't have to 'work', but that everything is in harmony and working together for good. Psalms such as 23, 37, and 145 capture this feeling. What characterises these Psalms in relation to our faith is the recognition of the goodness and faithfulness of God. They present the security and contentedness of order. Even when the Psalmist observes things out of order, such as the prospering of the wicked, they are not dis-orientated because they know that the "wicked will be cut down" (37:9). Order will eventually be restored.[19]

However when this harmony is interrupted, we experience feelings of dis-orientation. This is when difficult times hit. This is the season of pain and struggle. If orientation is heading in the right direction, then dis-orientation is being lost. It feels like the sky is falling. It might be an emotional or psychological dis-orientation. It might be a physical dis-orientation. It includes all facets of our experience.[20] It is at this time, as Brueggemann writes, that we are driven to the extremities of our emotions and of our language. This is when we have difficulty expressing our sense of loss or heartache. And it is in these situations that we struggle. In this struggle, we hope for a change for the better. We hope for a return to the former contentedness. These psalms are usually described as laments or complaints. They include psalms such as Psalms 22, 39, 56, 59 and 89. A lament is a heartfelt expression of grief or loss. These Psalms describe situations of distress. It is like the Psalmist opens the wounds of grief and despair to allow for the cleansing and healing process to begin to work. This process leads to reconciliation with God. As Psalm 42:5 cries: "Why are you cast down, O my soul? And why are you disquieted within me?" This psalm recognises that things are not right. The situation must change, and its God's obligation to change it. This is why they are appealing to God. Poems such as Psalm 109 look to God's justice where human justice has failed.

The psalms of dis-orientation provide an opportunity to let the language and imagery of the poem speak to people in this situation of confusion. For example, someone feeling abandoned by God will have no difficulty associating with Psalm 22. So these are important from a pastoral perspective. We can allow the words of the Psalmist to minister and resonate in the heart of people we are ministering to. The psalms truly do mirror our soul. It also helps the reader to verbalise their own frustrations and weaknesses.[21] However, while this is helpful, this reading of the Psalms is not an excuse for us to simply verbalise our grief and not address the situation at hand. Neither is it an excuse to express harm to another person. These are the verbalisation of thoughts to God alone. For example, Psalm 137 is what is called an 'imprecatory psalm'. These are poems that include harsh curses or calls for judgement against others. The Psalmist expresses to God their anger using language found in the covenant curses.[22] When there is injustice, we can take our concerns to God. However, as Christian readers we must read these through our Christ-coloured glasses that call us to the higher order of love.

What is perhaps most helpful about these psalms of dis-orientation is that there is generally a movement from grief to hope. In the midst of the pain, God answers. Although the circumstances may not be the same, God has spoken. It moves from despair and lament to faith and praise. So the Psalmist of chapter 22 shifts from abandonment to declaring God's praise in verse 17.[23] These psalms lead the reader to faith in God. They relate to the pain of the reader. But once they capture and verbalise this pain they walk through it to a new situation of hope and faith in God. Out of the struggle of dis-orientation, a new change comes. We see a light in the darkness. God breaks through. God delivers us. We are re-orientated. This makes the psalms of dis-orientation helpful in situations of grief and counselling.

The Psalmists turns from lament to thanksgiving. They give thanks to God for his goodness and faithfulness. These are often called 'psalms of thanksgiving'. They include Psalms such as 27, 33, 96, 128, and 131. They are different from the psalms of orientation in that they are giving immediate thanks. They thank God not just for the ongoing state of wellbeing but for a breakthrough. It is a new situation. This re-orientation is a gift from God – it was not achieved by human means. So this new circumstance results in praise and thanksgiving. Although the boat was going through the storm, it has come out into the sunshine. It represents a restoration. There is a restoration of confidence in God, of security, and of relationship. This model of orientation – dis-orientation – re-orientation is a good reminder that life is a journey in which we confront joy and pain and deliverance. Being believers doesn't exempt us from hurt, but offers us hope in God. We are offered the hope of deliverance, the hope of love, and the security in relationship with him. This also reflects the world-view of ancient Israel who perceived their life journey in these terms of crisis and deliverance. The example of the pattern of deliverance in the book of Judges is evidence of this as the people continually cycled through crisis to deliverance and salvation.

While many of the psalms are accredited to David, they actually were written by many different authors over different times. These were collected into what we now have as the book of Psalms. It is sometimes called the 'hymnbook' of ancient Israel. For the ancient Israelites, the psalms were centred in and around the Temple life. They would sing these songs in pilgrimage to the Temple as well as part of their worship once arrived. The Temple (located on Mt Zion) was the focus of these psalms. However, we can readily see the life and experiences of David reflected in some of the poetry of the Psalms and titles. During the period of David's reign (as well as his son Solomon's) there was a surge of interest in poetry, wisdom and philosophy. This was part of the economic growth and prosperity of this time. So while the psalms and 'wisdom literature' are not events that we can chart on a timeline, they are often equated with the golden period of Israel's history under the rulership of David and Solomon. In particular, Solomon was renowned for his wisdom (1 Kings 3: 16-28). This association of wisdom writings with royalty was also common throughout the ancient Near East.

There are three books of the Old Testament identified as 'Wisdom Literature'. These are Proverbs, Ecclesiastes and Job.[24] We often identify the wisdom writings of ancient Israel with the short, practical proverbs,[25] but actually there is much more to their wisdom. Wisdom in the Old Testament is more than knowledge of facts. It is the ability to take those facts and make them work in the world. As Fee and Stuart describe, wisdom is the discipline of applying truth to one's life in the light of experience.[26] There is an emphasis on practical knowledge, not just theory. The wise person knows when to speak and when to be silent. They also know how to act, not just when to act and when to be still. When temptation comes, they know how to act or respond. The wisdom writings teach the community to navigate life successfully.[27] This means that wisdom must be applied. As the sage Yoda from *Star Wars* might say: "Apply or not apply. There is no try".[28] It is not enough to memorise a proverb or read Ecclesiastes. Wisdom is actually about application. You must apply the proverb or knowledge correctly to the unique situation you face.

We often think of wisdom as being universal. We think of it as being some kind of absolute truth that will work in every situation. But when we look closely, particularly at Proverbs, it is very clearly situation specific. Proverbs, as part of wisdom literature, is context-sensitive.[29] The misapplication of proverbs is ridiculed in Proverbs 26:7: "in the mouth of a fool, a proverb becomes as limp as a paralysed leg" (TNIV). A paralysed leg is useless. It is almost a liability. This is what wisdom is like in the mouth of a fool. The fool knew the proverb, but didn't have wisdom to apply it properly.[30] The importance of context shows us why we sometimes have seemingly contradictory advice in the book. For example, Proverbs 26:4-5 seems to be suggesting contradictory behaviour. It tells you not to answer a fool, yet the very next verse tells you to answer one. What is one to do?

The wise person takes the context into consideration and responds appropriately.[31] The wise person reads the situation. Is this "fool" someone who is not willing to listen and unteachable? The first proverb would then apply. However, if the "fool" is someone who is willing to listen but needs instruction unless they think their silly idea is actually brilliant. Then they should be answered.[32] It recognises the complexities of life and the different situations we face. We need a wise answer for all of these situations. But that answer will be different according to the context. So wisdom is not just knowledge. Any "fool" can memorise a proverb or piece of poetry. Wisdom is the application of the proverb. Wisdom knows how to apply the proverb accurately. When it is applied correctly, then the wise person experiences success and peace.

However, this does not mean that the proverbs are simply a formula for success. The books of Job and Ecclesiastes provide a balance to this misconception. As Ecclesiastes 9:11 observes, at the end of the day it is not always the fastest runner who always win the race. The wise are often poor. Sometimes the wicked prosper (as expressed in the wisdom poetry of Psalm 73). The writings of Job and Ecclesiastes question the simplistic notion of wisdom that a reading of Proverbs alone can suggest. Why do good people suffer? This is a question encountered in a reading of Job. The book questions the logic that good things only happen to good people. To simply say that God blesses the righteous and curses the wicked is too simplistic, just as sowing a seed does not guarantee reaping a harvest. Job is innocent, yet he suffers. Although he is counselled by his "friends" to confess his sins, he continues to voice his innocence and frustration. The book however, at the core, questions the motivation of readers. Does Job only serve God because of the benefits? Is he faithful to God because of self-interest? In our contemporary context we may also ask: do we give because we will be blessed?

Despite this, the wisdom writings look to God as the answer. Although the wicked may prosper short-term, in the end, God does reward righteousness. It takes an eternal perspective (Psalm 1:5; 73:18-20). The wicked will reap their just rewards. There is an order to the world, and we must live by that order. In this sense, the wisdom literature of ancient Israel emphasises God as creator.

It recognises that God sustains the world he created. There are laws God has established in the world (such as sowing and reaping) that can be observed and followed. That order is guaranteed and sustained by God.[33] This doesn't mean that the wisdom literature of the Old Testament is 'secular' or not interested in covenant, but that it assumes good relationship with God.

However while the wisdom literature of ancient Israel does not explicitly refer to the Sinai covenant or the law, it upholds it. There is a link between wisdom and moral action.[34] The way of wisdom leads to prosperity in life and relationship with the Lord. This includes moral actions such as the repeated warnings against adultery and encouragements to be kind to the poor. So while the law and covenant will encourage moral action by commands such as: "Do not…commit adultery", wisdom literature is more likely to challenge the character. It doesn't just prohibit sin, but challenges the character and motivation that leads to sin. So wisdom is linked to the ethical behaviour outlined in the law. It also assumes the exclusive covenant loyalty outlined in the law. As Proverbs 1:7 notes, the fear of the Lord is the beginning of knowledge. Readers must choose relationship with God to choose wisdom. This is particularly emphasised in the presentation of 'wisdom' personified as a woman.

The first nine chapters of Proverbs confront the reader with a basic choice between a relationship with Lady Wisdom (who represents God himself) and one with Lady Folly (who represents idolatry). We are first introduced to Lady Wisdom in Proverbs 1:20. She calls to all the simple and immature to enter into an intimate relationship with her. As Tremper Longman notes, this metaphor will have the strongest impact if we remember the intended audience of the book. It was intended to be read by the young men of the ancient Israelite community (Proverbs 1:8; 2:1).[35] So the writer is trying to capture the attention of the young men. To do this, they use an image that will appeal to young men - a beautiful woman. However, Lady Wisdom is not the only person that the young man will meet.[36] He will also meet another woman (Lady Folly) who reaches out for a relationship him. Both women are trying to capture the attention of the young man. This is every young man's fantasy!

In Proverbs 9:4-12, Lady Wisdom finally invites the young man to a meal. This is not dinner with her parents - this is a fellowship meal. It is an intimate sign of fellowship. Longman highlights that the key to understanding this passage is in the location of the woman and her house. Her house is on the "heights overlooking the city" (9:3). She is located at the highest point in the city. In the ancient Near East world,[37] this was always the location of the Temple. So the image presents an invitation to intimate fellowship and worship.[38] As Lady Wisdom represents God, she is inviting the young man into fellowship with God. This is the heart of true wisdom. It is relationship with God. It results in life. Lady Folly also invites the young man to a fellowship meal (Proverbs 9:13-18). Her house is also located at the highest point of the city (9:14). She represents the worship of false gods.[39] Her meal is secret and stolen. It results in death. Which invitation will the young man choose? As contemporary readers, we also have a choice to embrace relationship with God or follow the path of our own way. So adopting the knowledge of Proverbs is more than just good advice, it is a theological statement. Being wise is not learning a pile of sayings. It is actually a relationship with God.

Let's consider the significance of this passage of Proverbs 9:1-18 using the tools of our trade. How is this passage significant to *them, us & me*?

The significance to *them* is:

- This passage was written to encourage the "son" to embrace the wisdom of God. It appeals to the young man through poetry. The inexperienced young man is about to make some big decisions in life. This includes finding a wife and starting a home.[40] This poem particularly uses an image relevant to a young man in this stage of his life. It uses an image of two women who represent the choices in life the young man will have to make

- Lady Wisdom represents God. She invites the young man to a fellowship meal. To enter her home above the city is to enter into fellowship with God. It is part of the covenant. By entering into a relationship with God, the young man not only demonstrates wisdom but is set on the pathway of learning true, life-giving wisdom

- Lady Wisdom is contrasted with Lady Folly. She also invites the young man to a fellowship meal. To enter her home above the city is to enter into fellowship with all the gods of the other nations. She represents idolatry. She may offer brief and dangerous excitement, but there is no future with her. By entering into a relationship with Lady Folly, the young man not only demonstrates foolishness but is set on the pathway of learning death-giving wisdom

- The young man (the reader) has a choice. In the journey of life he can choose the path of wisdom (God) or the path of folly (idolatry)

The significance to *us* is:

- Jesus Christ came from this people of ancient Israel

- Among other things, Jesus was a great wisdom teacher, speaking through parables and proverbs (such as Matthew 6:25-34). He is called in Luke 11:31 one greater than Solomon

- However, Jesus not only taught wisdom, but is wisdom personified. Like Lady Wisdom, Jesus ate with the sinners and fools as he invited them to follow in his way (Matthew 11:18-19). In John 14:6 Jesus identifies himself as called the "way, the truth and the life". Relationship with the Father is only through faith in him. Similarly, in 1 Corinthians 1:30, Jesus is described as wisdom incarnate (see also Colossians 2:3)[41]

- We follow the wisdom of Christ by following his teachings and example

- Jesus Christ inaugurates a new "way" of life and worship for the people of God in the New Testament. We don't have to go to a physical house to meet with God (such as Temple), but can fellowship with God anywhere

Although this will be different for each reader, **the significance to** *me* is:

- As a young woman, I am making important decisions in my journey through life. I need to embrace Christ as the way and the guidance for my life

- I need humility to walk this path so I don't become arrogant like the mocker in verse 8 or trust in my own wisdom, which is like embracing folly

As I embrace the wisdom of the bible I can be equipped to navigate life. However ancient Israel did not always follow their own good advice. Often they turned away from the wisdom of the prophets to follow their own pathway independent of God. This choice was disastrous. It led ultimately to their exile from the land - as we will see in the next chapter. It is to the destiny of Judah that we now return.

GROUP DISCUSSION QUESTIONS:

1. What is wisdom?

2. What is the main idea of the Psalms?

3. How are the Psalms similar to Proverbs?

4. Read Psalm 22. Apply the 'tools of the trade' to this passage:

    i. What is the significance to *them*?

ii. What is the significance to *us*?

iii. What is the significance to *me*?

RECOMMENDED READING

⅋ Longman, Tremper, *How to Read the Psalms*, (Downers Grove: IVP, 1988)

The 'How to Read..' series by Longman is particularly excellent. This is the first in the series (followed by Proverbs and Genesis). It is easy to read, practical and very profound.

⅋ Brown, William P. *Character in Crisis: A Fresh Approach to the Wisdom Literature of the Old Testament*, (Grand Rapids: Eerdmans), 1996

This is a useful introduction to the wisdom literature. It gives an overview of each book through the lens of the importance of character.

ENDNOTES:

1. Longman, T., *Making Sense of the Old Testament: Three Crucial Questions*, (Grand Rapids, Michigan: Baker, 1998), p.15

2. This is not to suggest that Santa Claus is real or even helpful to the Christmas message. Often the image and concept of Santa Claus is counter-productive to the purpose of Christmas. And, personally, I know he is not alive because I have seen the bones of St Nicholas in a cathedral in Bari, Italy!!

3. Consider as well the language used in the New Testament to describe their experience on the Day of Pentecost (Acts 2). They draw from Joel 2:28-32. The images from Joel are of the in-breaking of God into the natural realm that cannot contain his presence. So he describes blood, fire and smoke. These images point to God's presence. They are not literal. The Day of Pentecost and the coming of the Spirit represented a new work of God and the in-breaking of God into the natural realm. The Spirit had come to all believers. So this language from Joel was adopted by Peter to attempt to describe this experience of God.

4. MacFague, S., *Models of God: Theology for an Ecological Nuclear Age*, (London: SCM Press, 1987), p.33.

5. MacFague, S., *Models of God: Theology for an Ecological Nuclear Age*, p.33.

6. MacFague, S., *Models of God: Theology for an Ecological Nuclear Age*, p.39.

7. MacFague, S., *Models of God: Theology for an Ecological Nuclear Age*, p.39.

8. Brettler, M.Z., 'Incompatible Metaphors for Yhwh in Isaiah 40-66' *JSOT*, VOl 78, 1998, pp.97-120

9. Longman, T., *How to Read the Psalms*, (Downers Grove: IVP, 1988), p.117.

10. Longman, T., *How to Read the Psalms*, (Downers Grove: IVP, 1988), p.93.

11. Fee, G. D., & Stuart, D., *How to Read the Bible For all its Worth*, 3rd Ed., (Grand Rapids: Zondervan, 2003), p.171

12. Longman, T., *How to Read the Psalms*, (Downers Grove: IVP, 1988), p.98.

13. Longman, T., *How to Read Proverbs*, (Downers Grove: IVP, 2002), p.47.

14. Fee, G. D., & Stuart, D., *How to Read the Bible For all its Worth*, 3rd Ed., p.169

15. Longman, T., *How to Read the Psalms*, (Downers Grove: IVP, 1988), p.13.

16. Brueggemann, W., *The Psalms and the Life of Faith*, in Miller, P.D. (eds), (Minneapolis: Fortress, 1995), p.8

17. Brueggemann, W., *The Psalms and the Life of Faith*, p.9

18. Brueggemann, W., *The Psalms and the Life of Faith*, p.10

19. Brueggemann, W., *The Psalms and the Life of Faith*, p.10

20. Brueggemann, W., *The Psalms and the Life of Faith*, p.11

21. Brueggemann, W., *The Psalms and the Life of Faith*, p.27

22. Fee, G. D., & Stuart, D., *How to Read the Bible For all its Worth*, 3rd Ed., p.221

23. There is however, one exception – Ps 88. It is the only Psalm of disorientation that does not move to praise, but stays in that place of darkness (so to speak). So it doesn't move toward hope, but stays in hopelessness. It is the exception; all other Psalms of disorientation have this movement from hopelessness to hope.

24. Also some Psalms are also classified as 'wisdom psalms', such as Psalm 1

25. Longman, T., *How to Read Proverbs*, (Downers Grove: IVP, 2002), p.37

26. Fee, G. D., & Stuart, D., *How to Read the Bible For all its Worth*, 3rd Ed., p.187

27. Longman, T., *Making Sense of the Old Testament: Three Crucial Questions*, p. 131

28. Yoda actually says "Do or not do. There is no try". I think that Yoda is very similar to the idea of a sage in the ancient Near East.

29. Longman, T., *Making Sense of the Old Testament: Three Crucial Questions*, p.133

30. Longman, T., *How to Read Proverbs*, p.50

31. Longman, T., *How to Read Proverbs*, p.56

32. Longman, T., *How to Read Proverbs*, p.56

33. Murphy, R. E., *The Tree of Life*, (New York: Doubleday), 1990, p.115

34. Murphy, R. E., *The Tree of Life*, p.124

35. Longman, T., *How to Read Proverbs*, p.19

36. Longman, T., *How to Read Proverbs*, p.29

37. Longman, T., *How to Read Proverbs*, p.33

38. Longman, T., *How to Read Proverbs*, p.30

39. Longman, T., *How to Read Proverbs*, p.33

40. Clifford, R.J., *The Wisdom Literature*, (Nashville: Abingdon, 1998), p.56

41. Longman, T., *How to Read Proverbs*, p.107

Chapter 13

EXILE AND BACK

The writings and testimony of ancient Israel are very varied. In our study of the 'big picture' we have seen how these writings began with the narratives of creation. The hope for redemption became centred on Abraham and his family (in the 'patriarchal narratives'). They were chosen to be in a special covenant relationship with God. Whilst in Egypt, this family became enslaved. They cried out to God. God remembered his covenant and delivered them. Through a powerful confrontation, God redeemed them and led them through the desert to Sinai. Here as a nation group they were identified as God's special people. They formalised their relationship with God in the Sinai covenant (or Mosaic covenant). This established their rules for living in community through the law. The 'law' is another style of writing. The law included guidelines for their worship of God. They promised to be loyal to this redeeming God.

The people were led into the land of promise. This was described through another style of writing known as 'historical narrative'. Once the territory was conquered, they allocated land according to their tribes. During this time they were led by the Judges. However the people of the land (Canaan) had not been completely removed. This meant that the ancient Israelites were continually tempted to adopt the gods of these other people. The instability of the charismatic leadership and the military threat of the Philistines led the people to ask for a king. This was established under David, who united the nation. It was a time of prosperity. It was the golden age of poetry and 'wisdom literature'. However the

unity soon proved superficial as the nation divided. They became the
two kingdoms of the north (Israel or Ephraim) and south (Judah).
While the northern kingdoms had a variety of dynasties, there was
political stability in the south through the Davidic heir. Throughout
this time, the words of the prophets were recorded. Some of these
were woven into the historical narrative. Some of these were collected
and recorded separately in the books known as 'prophetic literature'.
Eventually however, both these kingdoms of ancient Israel became
embroiled in the wider politics of their time.

The northern kingdom wanted to be independent of the
domination of the Assyrians (as noted in chapter 11). So they led
a rebellion. They wanted Judah to join them. However, Judah's
king (Ahaz) refused. As such, the northern kingdom attacked the
southern kingdom. In this crisis, Ahaz called on Assyria to save them.
The Assyrians swiftly broke up the siege and later conquered the
northern kingdom, sending them into exile in 721 BCE. This ended
the testimony of the northern kingdom in our Old Testament text.
However the biblical text is clear that this exile occurred because of
the sins of the people (2 Kings 17:7). It was not because God was not
powerful enough to save them. On the contrary, according to the
covenant law, God was fighting against ancient Israel and ensuring
the success of Assyria. Assyria became the tool of God's just anger for
the sins of the people.

This left Judah alone and vulnerable. They were a vassal of
Assyria and about to be swept into a political power struggle between
the older supremacy of Assyria and the rising influence of Babylon.
Yet, between the exile of the northern kingdom in 721BCE and
the exile of the southern kingdom in 587BCE, there were pockets
of hope. This was offered primarily by the kings Hezekiah and
Josiah. If Ahaz was seen to be a weak king who was frightened into
becoming a vassal of Assyria, his son Hezekiah was the opposite. He
was examined as a good king as measured next to David in 2 Kings
18:1-8. In this passage, Hezekiah is particularly praised because of

his attitude to Assyria.[1] He destroyed the local shrines and purified Judah's worship. These actions had major political implications. Religion and politics were inter-related. To declare independent worship was to declare political independence. So while Assyria was busy dealing with other insubordinate nations, Hezekiah was able to consolidate Judah to prepare for the repercussions of his religious reforms.

This unrest was not unique to Judah. At this time in 705 BCE within the ancient Near East there was a general revolution breaking out against Assyria. Nations such as Egypt and Babylon were stirring the rebellion. When all of Judah's neighbours were rebelling, Hezekiah could not resist joining them. Despite the advice of the prophet Isaiah, Hezekiah adopted a complicated policy of alliances with Egypt and Babylon. Isaiah protested this involvement and counselled Hezekiah to stay out of the revolution. He called the political alliance against Assyria a "covenant with death" (Is 28:18). In particular, Isaiah condemned the alliance with Egypt (Isaiah 31:1-3). This was not because God was against their move for independence from Assyria, but was against them making alliances without consulting him. Hezekiah was putting his trust in the power of Egypt, not God. Again, Isaiah emphasised that Judah's hope was not in their shrewdness of politics, but in trusting God.

Sennacherib, ruler of Assyria, moved quickly to squash the rebellion. The Assyrian army marched through Babylon and into Judah in 701BCE. According to Sennacherib's account (the Assyrian version) he captured 46 of Hezekiah's fortified cities.[2] Anderson points out that the report in 2 Kings 18:13-16 generally agrees with this description.[3] Jerusalem was cut off from all outside help. According to Sennacherib's account, he shut up Hezekiah like a caged bird. Assyria did not completely destroy Jerusalem, but sent an ambassador to negotiate the terms of surrender. Then came the surprise. Isaiah had previously been counselling Judah not to revolt from Assyria. He considered Assyria to be the rod of God's anger. But now, Isaiah was counselling them to hold tight – to not to surrender to them (Isaiah 36-67 and 2 Kings 18:17-19).[4] Why did he change his mind? His perspective was not political but religious. Just like his message to Ahaz, Isaiah gave Hezekiah a "sign" that after three years they would return to sowing and reaping (37:30). In other words, if they held on, they would return to normality. Unlike Ahaz, Hezekiah responded to the prophetic word with faith. This sign was realised when Sennacherib suddenly withdrew. One of the accounts accredits this withdrawal to an angel of God destroying the enemy in their sleep.

This reign of Hezekiah was followed by probably one of the darkest moments in Judah's history. The reigns of Manasseh and his son Amon were particularly abominable in their practice of child sacrifice and divination (2 Kings 21). These heirs of David rebuilt all the high places (where idolatry was practiced) that Hezekiah had pulled down. Amon was assassinated after only two years on the throne. He was succeeded by Josiah, who was eight years old when he came to power. During these early years of Josiah, the supremacy of Assyria was on the decline. They were weakening. They had bigger concerns than this small and seemingly insignificant nation of Judah. This helped fuel the renewed nationalistic movement in Judah which blossomed at this time.[5] As politics and religion were inseparable in the ancient Near East, their increased political independence also meant religious independence.

This drive towards independence was probably already underway when a remarkable discovery was made in the eighteenth year of Josiah's reign. In 2 Kings 22 it tells us that when they were repairing the temple of Jerusalem, the "Book of the Covenant" was uncovered. While we are not sure exactly which book was found, many scholars think it was part (chapters 12-26) or all, of the book of Deuteronomy.[6] Josiah's response to the reading was to tear his clothes. This was a sign of repentance. He then led Judah in a renewal of the covenant. Josiah pledged to follow God and keep his commands with all his heart and all his soul. However it seemed that the reform only lasted as long as the political situation was favourable. Its easy to serve God when life is going well. Its even more attractive to 'serve' God if you think you will be blessed by it. Similarly, this is the complaint of Jeremiah against the people of Judah. Their hearts were not free from self-motivation.[7] According to the prophet Jeremiah, the renewal of the covenant did not result in a circumcision of the heart (Jer 10:16), but only produced nationalism and a twisting of the law. Like the challenge of the book of Job, Jeremiah questioned the motivations of people. Did they only serve God because of the benefits? The benefits of obedience were security in the land and good crops. Were they faithful to God because of self-interest? If they followed the law then they were ensured blessing. In the end the renewal did not bring the people what they expected. This is also a challenge for *us* in our service and giving to God: are we free from self-motivation?

During this time in the testimony of Judah, Assyria began to decline as the dominating force in the ancient Near Eastern. In this changing political climate, Josiah grew more bold. He moved to be free from the dominance of the hated Assyria. The prophecy of Nahum against Assyria reveals the pent-up anger and bitterness of Judah towards them. He spoke of the fall of Nineveh (which was the capital of Assyria) saying in 3:19: "Everyone who hears the news about you claps his hands at your fall, for who has not felt your endless cruelty?" (TNIV). But what followed was a strange turn of events. Egypt who was Assyria's former enemy (and who Assyria had previously invaded) decided to help them. It seems (according to Egypt) a weak Assyria was better than the emerging force of Babylon. Egypt considered Babylon a more dangerous threat. As the saying goes: better the devil you know than the devil you don't! So Egypt went to the aid of a failing Assyria. However Josiah had a different political plan. He decided to align himself with the emerging Babylonians and throw off the shackles of Assyria. So Josiah attempted to intercept the Egyptian army at Meddigo. Josiah, not yet forty years old, was defeated and killed in battle by Egypt and Judah made a vassal. It is one of the most tragic moments in the history of ancient Israel. After Josiah, the fall of Jerusalem was inevitable. The rulers of Judah were basically vassals of Egypt.

The kings of Judah were under Egyptian control until the Pharaoh met his match in the Babylonian ruler, Nebuchadnezzar. This meant that after four years of Egyptian rule, the southern kingdom was now under Babylonian rule. Babylon was the undisputed super-power of the ancient Near Eastern world. As a vassal of the defeated Egypt, Jehoiakim, king of Judah, had to pledge allegiance to Nebuchadnezzar. However Jehoiakim rebelled. The response of Babylon was swift. They marched against Judah, with the aid of Judah's neighbours Syria, Moab and Ammon. They defeated the southern kingdom.

Yet the flames of rebellion still burned in the last ruler, Zedekiah. He refused to pay tribute to Babylon. The response of Nebuchadnezzar was swift (yet again). He marched against Jerusalem and besieged it for two years. If Zedekiah was waiting for the destroying angel of God to come like in Hezekiah's day, he was mistaken. Eventually, in 587BCE, Jerusalem was taken. The city was burnt and levelled. Zedekiah witnessed the murder of his sons, was blinded and marched into captivity to Babylon. The people in the city were taken into exile while the rural peasantry remained. And as 2 Kings 25:21 records: "So Judah went into captivity, away from her land" (TNIV). So the historical narratives or former prophets finish their testimony in exile. Many of the laments in the book of Psalms (such as Ps 137) and the book of Lamentations record the loss and despair of the people. The people had lost the temple, the place of God's presence. They had lost their land, the sign of God's concrete blessing on them. They were defeated.

Throughout this time, the prophets had spoken to the people to remind them of their responsibility to abide by the covenant. Because of the failure of the people to obey the covenant, a lot of what appears in the prophetic books were warnings of the negative consequences of failing to obey. Time and time again through the prophets, God warned the people of the curses he would be forced to impose (see Jeremiah 25:8-9). Although hoping for signs of repentance from the people, they did not listen. So the ultimate curse of the covenant came upon them – exile. While the threat of exile was continually announced by the prophets, it seems the people did not think it would be a possibility. They were the people of God. They had the Temple. How could God allow this? Yet, the reflections of their historians (the Former Prophets) came to the conclusion that the exile did not occur not because God was less powerful than Marduk (the principle Babylonian god). The exile occurred because they had sinned against God. They had not kept the covenant, so the justice of God was forced to inflict this punishment. If not, God would not be faithful. However, a theme developed through the prophets of Judah leading up to the exile (such as Isaiah and Jeremiah) and during it (such as Ezekiel). Although there was impending punishment, there was also a promised remnant (Isaiah 6:13). God would show his grace in leaving a remnant – a group of people who would survive the exile and continue as the people of God. In this remnant was the hope of the nation. It was the hope of restoration. They would not be forgotten by God, but eventually restored. From this remnant, the greatest hope - Jesus Christ- came.

The question that Judah faced in the exile was: Was this the end? Could they survive as a nation? *How* could they survive? Their land was decimated, their city destroyed and the Temple was ruined. The exile was a major threat to the distinctiveness of the faith of ancient Israel. As displaced people they could have just been absorbed into the religion, culture and society of Babylon. They could have assimilated. However they held onto their distinctiveness. The challenge throughout this period was: how do they remain the people of God outside the land. As Psalm 137 asks: how could they worship God in a strange land? They had no Temple, no evidence of God's presence. Were they still the people of God? If they could no longer worship and offer sacrifices in the temple, how could they follow God? If they had no king to represent God, how could they be ruled by God? This was a crisis.

In their hopelessness, the prophets preached a message of hope and restoration. Like the valley of dry bones in Ezekiel 37:1-14, they would be restored to life. God had not forgotten them. Let's consider this passage from Ezekiel a little more closely. Take a moment to read Ezekiel 37: 1-14 using the tools of our trade. How is this passage significant to *them, us* & *me*?

The significance to *them* is:

- It is the record of the prophetic vision received by Ezekiel during the time of exile

- It captures the hopelessness of the situation and the feeling of the people removed from their land. The people feel like hopeless, dry bones with no hint of life. It offers the hope of restoration

- The prophet is the agent of God to speak life and hope to their situation

- In this vision, as the prophet speaks the Spirit works to restore life. This is different to the Spirit at creation where God spoke and the Spirit moved. Now God works through the prophet to speak the divine word. When the prophet speaks the word of God, then the Spirit moves

- The Spirit will be active in the restoration (depicted as a resurrection) of the nation

The significance to *us* is:

- From this people, Jesus Christ would come

- Jesus took our sin. However he conquered death and was resurrected

- This vision offers a picture of the salvation found in Jesus Christ. We were dead in our sin but Christ has resurrected us and restored us. While we are saved, we await the final work of salvation in the final resurrection from the dead

- Like the prophet, the church is active to promote the message of Jesus that offers this salvation

Although this will be different for each reader, **the significance to** *me* is:

- This passage particularly speaks to me about the role of each of us as prophets. It is not just special people who have this ministry but all believers. This includes me. As Ezekiel spoke the word of God then the Spirit moved. So I also have a role and responsibility to speak the word of God. As I do, the Spirit will be at work. God works through me. I am called to partner with God to speak life and hope to people

Although Judah had been taken captive by Babylon, the new Babylonian empire did not last long after the reign of Nebuchadnezzar. They were overpowered by the strength of Persia led by Cyrus. His approach to governing his vassals was to allow their local governments to control their own domain while exacting tribute money. His approach and attitude was quite humane toward the conquered peoples. He respected the forms of religion of the different people groups and even permitted exiles to return to their homelands. In particular, he allowed the Judeans (now called the 'Jews', or sometimes now 'Israel' by the prophets) to return to their homeland. So with Cyrus we see the beginning of the Persian Empire, which would last for two hundred years until the rise of Alexander the Great.

Cyrus permitted deported groups to return to their homeland. He considered himself to be the patron of the gods of all the conquered peoples. He supported the restoration of their temples, including the Temple of Jerusalem which was rebuilt with support from the Persian treasury as Ezra 6 describes. He even allowed for the restoration of the utensils of worship from the Temple that Nebuchadnezzar had taken (Ezra 1:7-11). If the prophets saw Assyria and Babylon as tools of God's judgement, so Isaiah saw Cyrus as a tool of God's restoration (Is 45:9-13). The biblical history of this period is found in the two books of Ezra and Nehemiah. However, despite this goodwill of Cyrus, he was still the overlord of Judah. They were not free and independent, but subjects of a foreign power. The monarchy of the pre-exilic days was not restored. It looked like it would never be restored. Their only hope for a return to the 'golden days' of David was in the expectation of a future messiah. Many Jews, who do not recognise Jesus Christ, still wait for this messiah.

The restoration of the nation and return to the land was likened by some of the prophets to a second exodus. Just as Israel exited Egypt from a position of slavery to be liberated into land of their own, so God promised them a second exodus from exile. They would be re-established in the land. The 'prophetic literature' of Isaiah 40-55 is filled with promises to the people about their restoration. The proclamation is centred around "homecoming".[8] It speaks comfort to the people that they have paid for their sins. It is now time to return home. The prophet envisions a great procession led by God as the exiled Jews would march home. God would lead them through the desert as he did at the first exodus. God would provide for them a safe journey, a journey where the mountains will be levelled for his people to march through triumphantly returning to their land (Isaiah 40:1-5). The same God that brought them out of slavery once, can do it again. God can carry them, once again, on the wings of eagles.

So while the return from exile was pictured by the prophets as a second exodus, the reality of their return was not quite so majestic. It was more of a filtering than a mass migration. This return from exile was not the golden age ancient Israel had expected or hoped for. Many Judeans chose not to return to the land but to stay in

their new homes around Mesopotamia and Egypt (such as Esther).
Yet, even with the small number of returnees the community that
had remained in Judah struggled to accommodate the influx of
refugees. They were a strain on the resources of a community already
barely surviving in the decimated land. However the stress on the
re-forming community was more than economic. There were also
political tensions.

In the Babylonian blitz, it was the leaders and aristocracy
who had been taken captive and exiled to the foreign land. This was
their judgement, such as that predicted by Isaiah in the Song of the
Vineyard (Isaiah 5). The people left behind were the peasantry and
lower classes. However in the absence of the royal leadership, the
governmental positions had been filled by the remaining community
members. So when the exiles returned, they wanted to return to their
previous roles and vocations. In their view, they were the legitimate
rulers of Judah. Those exiled identified themselves as the "true"
Israel, or the "good figs" of Jeremiah's vision (Jer 24). They had the
authority from Persia to rebuild. They were appointed to govern
by the Persian government. Figures such as Ezra and Nehemiah
represent these returning elite. That there would be tension between
the two groups is understandable. This caused great pressure on the
re-forming community. This internal disunity was also intensified
by the external hostility of the neighbouring people (such as that
described in Nehemiah).

Despite this struggle, the people united to rebuild the land.
Under the Davidic leadership of Sheshbazzar, the Judeans began to
lay the foundations for the Temple in Jerusalem. Ezra 5:1 records that
this work was encouraged by two prophets: Haggai and Zechariah.
It was, as Zechariah describes, "a day of small things" (Zech 4:10)
especially in comparison to the Temple of Solomon that had been
very grand and exquisitely built. When the older priests and family
heads that had seen the former Temple saw the foundations, they wept
(Ezra 3:12). After the laying of this foundation and the establishing

of basic shrines, it seems the people became discouraged. This was typified by men divorcing their wives to marry foreign women, and "robbing God" by not paying their tithes and offerings (Malachi 1-3). Particularly, the next governor Zerubbabel and high priest Joshua, were inspired by the ministry of Haggai and Zechariah to mobilise the community to complete the building. It took approximately twenty years to complete. This Temple became known as the Second Temple. However, this Second Temple seemed hollow. There was no shekinah cloud and glory like at the dedication of Solomon's temple. There was no sense that God's presence had returned. Although synagogues were later established in Jewish communities outside Jerusalem in the Diaspora (or dispersion), the Temple was still the centre of Jewish life and the place of pilgrimage for devout Jews.[9] The people renewed the sacrificial system, but it was not the same. Approximately a generation later, under the leadership of Nehemiah, the city walls would be rebuilt. Yet even amidst the hostility of the neighbouring people, the book of Nehemiah records how the people of Jerusalem persevered. They re-built the city walls with a tool in one hand and a sword in the other.

Yet, discouragement and disunity continued to mark the re-forming community. They faced not only economic and political stress, but also a religious crisis. Were the people living outside of the land included in this group called 'people of God'? How were they to define the 'people of God' in this new context? For example, the law given in the Sinai covenant prohibited any eunuch to enter the Temple area (Deuteronomy 23: 1-3). In its context of pre-exile, this would mainly been referring to foreigners. However in this new context of post-exilic Judah (or Second Temple Judaism as it is commonly referred to), the situation had changed. Some of the Judeans would have been forced to become eunuchs by the Babylonian and Persian court where they served as court officials (probably similar to Daniel). What were the people to do? How were the people of God to interpret the law in this new setting? According to Isaiah 56, a new reading of the law was needed. This was a unique situation and required the unique guidance of God. Isaiah 56 promises those eunuchs who hold fast to the covenant, that God would give them a memorial and a name better than children (56:4-5).

However the most threatening dilemma to their faithfulness to the law came with the issue of inter-marriage. The re-forming community had to face the issue of their inter-marriage. Many of the Judeans had married foreign wives. However unlike Ruth, these women were not converts but were leading the children (as well as husbands) away from the Jewish faith. The response of Nehemiah to this situation demanded strict obedience to the law. The foreign wives would be dismissed and the children taught the language of Judah (Hebrew). This was a policy of exclusivity aimed at establishing Jewish purity and keeping a distinct Jewish identity (Nehemiah 13:23-31). Considering their context, this approach is understandable. Why had they been exiled? They had been exiled for their failure to keep the law. Inter-marriage was prohibited by the law (Deuteronomy 7:3-4). However there were alternative approaches. There were alternative voices within the community as they attempted to forge a new life. Isaiah offered what some scholars refer to as a new universalism, or a new inclusiveness.[10] It invited foreigners to join the community (Isaiah 56:1-8). However, the invitation assumed that these foreigners had taken on the faith of ancient Israel. Yet, it highlights that this was not a uniform community. We sometimes think of the books of the Old Testament as providing a unified voice. There were however competing voices and alternative ideas. The dilemma of this re-forming community reminds us that real community is not found in uniformity (homogeny). Real unity emerges in the midst of dialogue and diversity.

The challenge of this new context forced the community to re-think the boundaries of inclusion. The details of this issue were never fully resolved. However there was a general acceptance that developed. The people of God did not have to live in the land. They could practice their faith in any geographic location. However, they must worship God alone. This definition of the people of God and requirement came to be known as 'Judaism'. However, the community represented by that name (Judaism) was not uniform. By the time of Jesus in the first-century these many competing voices had formed doctrines (such as the theology and practices of the Pharisees, Sadducees, etc) and sub-groups within the Jewish community. In the next chapter, we will briefly examine the development of the Jewish community to the time of Christ.

GROUP DISCUSSION QUESTIONS:

1. What has happened in the testimony of ancient Israel from creation up to this point (Second Temple period)? In your group, make a time-line of the major events. Include in this time-line when the individual prophets were active.

2. Why did the exile occur? How would you feel if you were one of the exiles?

3. What were some of the challenges for the re-forming community after the exile?

4. Read Joel 2:28-32. Apply the 'tools of the trade' to this passage:

   i. What is the significance to *them*?

   ii. What is the significance to *us*?

   iii. What is the significance to *me*?

ENDNOTES:

1. Anderson, B.W., *The Living World of the Old Testament*, 4th Ed, (Essex: Longman, 1990), p.280.

2. Anderson, B.W., *The Living World of the Old Testament*, p.286.

3. Anderson, B.W., *The Living World of the Old Testament*, p.286.

4. Anderson, B.W., *The Living World of the Old Testament*, p.287.

5. Anderson, B.W., *The Living World of the Old Testament*, p.307.

6. Anderson, B.W., *The Living World of the Old Testament*, pp.309-314.

7. Anderson, B.W., *The Living World of the Old Testament*, pp.319-320.

8. Brueggemann, *Isaiah 40-66*, (Louisville, Kentucky: Westminster/John Knox Press, 1998), p.19.

9. Anderson, B.W., *The Living World of the Old Testament*, pp.438-440.

10. Brueggemann, *Isaiah 40-66*, p.165.

Chapter 14

CONCLUSION

The history and hope of the Jewish people did not switch off at Malachi. Their story did not suddenly disappear and then re-appear 400 years later with Jesus Christ. Between the Testaments is a history of intrigue, challenge and disappointed hopes. Some of the books from this period, such as the books of Maccabees and Judith are found in the Apocrypha (see chapter 2). This period is known as the Second Temple era. It generally refers to the time between the Babylonian destruction of the first Jerusalem temple (587 BCE.) and the Roman destruction of the second Jerusalem temple (70 CE.). Throughout this time, the ancient Israelites struggled to re-form their community. This was made difficult by the fact that much of the community remained outside the land. Although some of the people had returned to the land, many remained outside its geographic boundaries. There were significant Jewish communities in Mesopotamia and Egypt. Jerusalem was not the only centre for the developing ideas of Judaism. These other groups also contributed to the divergent ideas within the Jewish community. In particular, the Egyptian community in Alexandria contributed the translation of the scriptures into Greek (known as the Septuagint or LXX).

The community also struggled to re-form their worship. Although the temple had been rebuilt, the former glory had not returned. While worship was scattered throughout synagogues in these communities outside of Jerusalem,[1] the Temple was still the focus of devotion. Yet according to some of the post-exilic prophets, their worship was marked by indifference and unrighteousness. Although they continued to offer the sacrifices required by the law in Jerusalem, they were presenting blemished offerings (Malachi 1:6-14). Although the priests had initially returned to service, the people were not tithing which meant the priests could not fulfil their roles. Instead they turned to farming to survive (Malachi 3:6-17; Nehemiah 13:10-13). Despite the experience of the exile, it seemed that the people were not honouring the covenant.

This challenge of the exile redefined the Judean community. There was a sense that the exile was not over.[2] Despite this, those that could not worship in the temple in Jerusalem began to focus on the law. As noted in the last chapter, this became the expression of their covenant loyalty. It required their worship to be directed exclusively to God. The laws that could be practiced outside of the land became the identity markers within groups of Judaism. For some groups, this exclusive worship of God meant strict adherence to the dietary laws. For others, it included refusing food offered to idols. The figure of Daniel was an example of this identity marker in the court narratives (Daniel 1-6). While Daniel was taken into the service of a foreign king in a foreign land he submitted to most of the requirements of this new context. He was taken to the palace to be a court official. He learnt the language, philosophies and literature of this foreign land. He submitted to these roles. However he did not submit to eating the food and wine from the king's table. Why? They were offered to idols. It would be practising idolatry and a violation of 'torah'. The book of Daniel offers encouragement to the struggling community to look to the ultimate deliverance of God.

Out of this new context of exile, a new development of prophecy emerged. The question of Psalm 137 at this time was: How can we sing the Lord's song in a foreign land?[3] As Witherington notes, the question raised by the prophets at this time was: How can we prophesy in a foreign land? Unlike the earlier prophets, the prophets of the Second Temple era had no king to address. Prophets like Ezekiel and Daniel were no longer in the holy land, except through what they could see in dreams and vision.[4] The new development of prophecy is called 'apocalyptic' (from the Greek word "revelation"). The purpose of apocalyptic literature is generally thought to be an encouragement to the faithful to persevere. The faithful must endure the present evil age until the decisive moment in history when God will act. The apocalyptic writers inherently believed that God would intervene in history to judge the world. However because they were under the domination (and sometimes persecution) of a foreign power, their message was coded in mythic language and imagery. Their visions were marked by angelic visitations and the expectation of a final judgement. The second half of Daniel represents this type of writing that developed.[5] It particularly flourished in the Hellenistic period.

After the exile, the ancient Israelites were no longer an independent nation. Although they were allowed some self-government, they were really colonies of Babylon - then Persia, Greece and Rome. There were many responses to this foreign domination. Part of this apocalyptic program of Second Temple Judaism was the belief that God would intervene in human history to defeat and punish their foreign overlords. This intervention could be done by God directly or indirectly through a human agent called a 'messiah'. The people looked for a messianic deliverer who would purge the land of the foreign powers. This deliverer would restore the nation so they could return to the 'golden era' of King David. The focus was on the restoration of the kingdom. The coming of this messiah would be prepared by a new Elijah. This idea was based on the text of Malachi which refers to a messenger who will prepare the way for God as the prophet Elijah (Mal 4:5-6). Aune notes that even in contemporary Jewish Passover celebrations a cup of wine is poured for Elijah and the door opened for his arrival.[6]

The Persian dominance of much of the ancient Near East was crushed by Alexander the Great. As Wright notes, he not only painted the map a new colour but also imposed a new culture.[7] The introduction of Greek (or Hellenistic) culture threatened the Jewish culture and religion. It became the dominant, common language (known as *koine* Greek) and provided a new world-view for the ancient Near East. Within ten years he had expanded his empire to the largest that the world had ever known. However Alexander was not particularly clear about who would replace him, so when he died at aged 33, his kingdom was divided between his generals. The most important of these to this study were Ptolemaic Egypt and Seleucid Syria. So for the next century, Palestine was under Ptolemaic rule. The challenge of Hellenism still provoked diverse responses within the scattered community. Some within Judaism attempted to reconcile the culture with their faith (such as Philo in Alexandria)[8] while others attempted to maintain a strict exclusivity.

In 199BCE the Seleucids seized control of Palestine. Led by Antiochus IV, they began to forcibly impose Greek culture onto the Jewish community. In particular, they banned the Sabbath, outlawed circumcision and desecrated the temple. Considering these were the main identity markers of the Jewish community it should come as no surprise that it produced a massive reaction. This persecution sparked a rebellion led by Judas Maccabaeus. Through this surprise revolt he liberated Jerusalem and restored temple worship. This story is recorded in the books of Maccabees. He established the Hasmonean dynasty. While the Maccabean revolt was crushed, the Hasmonean dynasty continued with the office of High Priest in partnership with the Seleucids. However it did not stop the unrest and dissatisfaction amongst the many sub-groups of Judaism with this foreign rule. There were numerous movements led by popular 'messianic' and 'prophetic' deliverers prior to and contemporary with the ministry of Jesus Christ. This rulership was eventually replaced by Rome when Pompey captured Jerusalem in 63BCE. This Roman rule lasted until the seventh century CE.[9]

It was into this religious, social and political context that Jesus Christ came. The majority of the Jewish believers in the first century were expecting a political deliverer to overthrow the foreign rulership. They were expecting the messiah to re-establish an independent state reflective of the glorious days of the united monarchy under David. Although ironically identified as the 'king of the Jews' at his crucifixion, Jesus Christ did not come to establish a political kingdom. Instead, he came to redefine it. Through the life and work of Jesus Christ, the rule of God is no longer a geographic, social or political entity. The parables of Jesus re-defined what this kingdom of God is like. It is like a father that graciously embraces the wayward and prodigal son (Luke 15:11-32). Though the law would require the father to condemn this son to death (Deuteronomy 21:18-21), the father chooses life for his son. The rule of God has been re-defined. This rule of God is now within the hearts of women and men across the world. This is where God reigns as king - in the hearts of believers. This kingdom is available to any who seek. Through Jesus Christ, the fractured relationship between God and humanity can be restored. It is restored in the hearts of believers. The Holy Spirit is given as a seal of our salvation (2 Corinthians 1:22).

Yet this work is not finished. It is still being restored in the hearts of believers. Paul reminds us to work out our salvation with fear and trembling (Philippians 2:12). We are saved, and yet, we are being saved. We are saved as individual Christians, yet we form the body of Christ. We form the body of Christ so we can demonstrate to those yet to be reconciled with God the nature and character of this God we love and serve. We are called to shine the character of God. As the special intent of God's creation we shine his image. As vassals in heartfelt response to our suzerain, we demonstrate God's grace in our interaction (John 14:15). By this, all people will know that we are the disciples of Jesus Christ, as we love one another (John 13:34-35). This is our purpose and hope. However, the Old Testament continually reminds us that salvation is not the exclusive domain of humanity. The whole creation awaits the salvation and redemption that we can find in Jesus Christ. We look forward to the culmination of this salvation begun by Christ. If you have not joined this community of salvation, the door is open to you now.

In offering this salvation, God has taken a thousand steps so that you need only take one. This is the same principle by which we understand the bible as the testimony of God's interaction with humanity. God has spoken to communities in the past. This is their record that has been handed to us. With these treasured words, we can understand God. We can understand the world God has created, and how we are meant to function in that world. The Christian life is a journey. Our discovery of God is a journey. Along the way, we need the words of our Old and New Testaments to help point us to God.

So while we have come to the end of the journey of this book, it is important to look back at where we have been. There have been two stages to our journey. The first stage was like preparing the luggage for our trip. We packed the equipment we would need for the journey. The necessary tools that we packed have been summarised into three questions:

1. What is the significance for *them?*
2. What is the significance for *us?*
3. What is the significance for *me?*

All three of these questions are vital for the journey. To ignore one is to dishonour the principle on which our bibles have been given to us. God speaks to each generation in a contemporary, fresh and meaningful way. If I just read the Old Testament for my personal insight and ignore what it has meant for its original community (*them*) or the community of Christ (*us*) then I am ignoring the purpose of God's word as a meaningful message to each of the hearers. Of these hearers, I am one of many. The Old Testament was a product of its time. It is a testimony that was written in a particular time and place. Sometimes I don't understand this world of the Old Testament. However that does not mean that I discard it. I look to others (through discussion or by reading books) to help me understand. I try and put on the sandals of their ancient culture to understand their world and context. I study it as part of my life-long journey. Through reading this treasured text I can know God better and allow God to speak into my life.

The second part of our journey involved travelling through the major events, concepts and writings of the Old Testament. This gave us the 'big picture' of their story. That story spanned hundreds of years. It tracked enormous social change from a nomadic family to urban dwellers. It also presented an ongoing revelation of the creator, redeemer, warrior, compassionate, just God. This revelation of God was recorded in diverse writings from narrative to law to poetry. Yet through it all, God was revealed to *them*. God was revealed through Christ for us. God was revealed for you and for me. I hope that you have been enriched by this journey. But it's not over yet! I hope that you continue this journey with the tools you have been given to keep reading, growing and loving God as you explore the Old Testament for yourself and as part of the body of Christ.

GROUP DISCUSSION QUESTIONS:

1. Describe the situation of the Jewish people in this 'Second Temple' period.

2. What questions would you ask of a Jewish person in this 'Second Temple' period?

3. How confident do you now feel at the conclusion of this journey to read the Old Testament on your own?

4. Read Malachi 4. Apply the 'tools of the trade' to this passage:

   i. What is the significance to *them*?
   ii. What is the significance to *us*?
   iii. What is the significance to *me*?

ENDNOTES:

1. Also called the Diaspora

2. This idea is developed by N.T Wright in his excellent book: *The New Testament and the People of God*, (SPCK, 1992).

3. Witherington, B. III, *Jesus the Seer: The Progress of Prophecy*, (Massachusetts: Hendrickson, 1999), p.145.

4. Witherington, B. III, *Jesus the Seer: The Progress of Prophecy*, p.145.

5. The Book of Revelation is an example of apocalyptic literature in the New Testament

6. Aune, D.E., *Prophecy in Early Christianity and the Ancient Mediterranean World*, (Grand Rapids: Eerdmans, 1983), p.124.

7. Wright, N.T., *The New Testament and the People of God*, (SPCK, 1992), p.156.

8. Charpentier, E., *How to Read the Bible: The Old and New Testaments*, (New York: Gramercy Books, 1981), p.84.

9. Charpentier, E., *How to Read the Bible: The Old and New Testaments*, p.85.

If you have never made a formal decision to be a follower of Jesus Christ, then now is the perfect time to begin. You just need to open your heart to God in prayer and accept Jesus into your heart. In doing this, you turn from your own means of salvation and the many times you have rejected God or his ways. However, the Christian walk is not a solo journey. It is important that you connect with other people with this same faith. I encourage you to find a local Christian church in which to connect to other Christians with whom you can share your journey.

INDEX